PART ONE

GATEWAY
to
TORAH

Book of Bereshit

by
MIRIAM LORBER and JUDITH SHAMIR

Torah Translation by
Arthur Chiel

KTAV PUBLISHING HOUSE INC.

CONTENTS

4

תַּנַ"ךְ
THE BIBLE

Can you think of one book that has changed the world? One book that has been read by millions and millions of people? One book that contains the wisdom of the ages—history, poetry, commandments and prayers, and sacred teachings? That one book is the Bible, the holiest book ever written. The Bible is considered holy by Jews, Christians, and Moslems alike. Because so many people want to read it and to learn from it, the Bible has been translated into more than 1,100 different languages. But no translation can compare to the original Hebrew. You see, each beautiful, poetic word of the Bible is filled with meaning. That is why so many commentaries have been written to explain the Bible.

In Hebrew, we call the Bible the תַּנַ"ךְ (Tanakh). The letters ךְ , נַ , and תַּ stand for the words תּוֹרָה (Torah), נְבִיאִים (N'vi'im), and כְּתוּבִים (K'tuvim). These are the names of the three types of books that make up the Bible. The Torah consists of the Five Books of Moses. N'vi'im are the books about prophets, great men who carried God's message to our people. K'tuvim are books of writings that are not about prophets. In all, there are 24 separate books in the Tanakh.

I. THE PENTATEUCH — THE TORAH
The Five Books of Moses

1. Genesis — Bereshit
2. Exodus — Shemot
3. Leviticus — Vayikra
4. Numbers — Bamidbar
5. Deuteronomy— Devarim

תּוֹרָה

THE TORAH

When we say "Bible," we often mean the *Torah*, the Five Books of Moses. These five holy books tell the ancient history of the Jewish people from the creation of the world up to the time we reached the Promised Land of Israel. They describe our customs and ceremonies, including the 613 *mitzvot* (commandments).

The Hebrew name for each of the five books is taken from the first meaningful word in that book. The first book, בְּרֵאשִׁית *(Bereshit)*, called *Genesis* in English, tells the story of the creation of the world and tells about our Matriarchs and our Patriarchs.

The second book, שְׁמוֹת *(Shemot)* called *Exodus* in English, describes the life of the Jews in Egypt and tells how they left Egypt and received the Ten Commandments at Mount Sinai. The third book, וַיִּקְרָא *(Vayikra)*, called *Leviticus* in English, lists the laws and work of the *kohanim* (priests) in the ancient Temple in Jerusalem and lists the laws of cleanliness. בַּמִּדְבָּר *(Bamidbar)*, the fourth book, called *Numbers* in English, tells the story of the wanderings of the Children of Israel for forty years in the desert. דְּבָרִים *(Devarim)*, or *Deuteronomy* in English, reviews the laws and commandments set down in the rest of the Torah.

Because the Torah contains so much beauty and wisdom in so short a space, it is difficult to know or understand all that the Torah has to teach us. Therefore, we read and study the Torah all the time. The Torah is read aloud in the synagogue three times a week. Each Sabbath a new portion or *sidrah* of the Torah is chanted. When we read the last portion on the holiday of *Simhat Torah*, Rejoicing with the Torah, we immediately begin again by reading the very first portion of the Torah too. This is our way of showing that you can never really finish the study of the Torah. There is always something new to be learned from it.

The Torah that we read in the synagogue is a scroll that has been hand-written by a scribe on parchment, not paper. It has no punctuation marks and no vowels, so you must know the Torah well before you can read it aloud in the synagogue. The Torah scrolls are kept in the אֲרוֹן הַקֹּדֶשׁ *(Aron Hakodesh)*, Holy Ark.

נְבִיאִים

THE PROPHETS

There are eight books about prophets in the Bible. Prophets were great men who had visions, special dreams in which God appeared to them and told them what He wanted the Children of Israel to do. The prophets brought God's message to the people. Often the message was a reminder to live by the laws of the Torah, to be kind and fair with one another. Perhaps the best-known prophet is Isaiah. Isaiah promised the Children of Israel that if they were careful to do good, they would be rewarded with peace. a world in which the wolf and the lamb could live together.

The books of the Prophets are divided into Early Prophets, books about prophets who lived at an earlier time, and Later Prophets, books about prophets who lived in a later period. The Early Prophets are: *Joshua, Judges, Samuel I and II, Kings I and II.* The Later Prophets are: *Isaiah, Jeremiah, Ezekiel,* and *T'rei Asar (Twelve Minor Prophets).* The stories of the twelve minor prophets are too short to stand alone, so they are grouped into one book.

II. THE PROPHETS —
a. Early Prophets —

1.	Joshua	— Yehoshua
2.	Judges	— Shofetim
3.	Samuel, I	— Shemuel, Aleph
	Samuel, II	— Shemuel, Bet
4.	Kings, I	— Melakhim, Aleph
	Kings, II	— Melakhim, Bet

b. Later Prophets —
The Three Major Prophets:

Isaiah	— Yeshayah
Jeremiah	— Yirmeyah
Ezekiel	— Yehezkeel

The Twelve (Minor) Prophets —

Hosea	— Hoshea
Joel	— Yoel
Amos	— Amos
Obadiah	— Ovadyah
Jonah	— Yonah
Micah	— Mikha
Nahum	— Nahum
Habakkuk	— Habakkuk
Zephaniah	— Zephanyah
Haggai	— Haggai
Zechariah	— Zekhariah
Malachi	— Malakhi

כְּתוּבִים

THE HOLY WRITINGS

The *K'tuvim*, or *Holy Writings*, are eleven sacred books on different subjects. There are three books of poetry: *Psalms*, *Proverbs*, and *Job*. The book of *Psalms* contains beautiful songs and prayers. The book of *Proverbs* gives us lessons for daily living. The book of *Job* is a story that teaches us that we should have faith in God.

K'tuvim also contains five scrolls: *Song of Songs*, *Ruth*, *Lamentations*, *Ecclesiastes*, and *Esther*. *Ruth* and *Esther* tell the stories of great Jewish heroines. *Ruth* teaches us to be loyal to each other and to our religion. *Esther* tells us how a brave woman saved all the Jews in Persia. The *Song of Songs* is a book of poetry written by King Solomon. *Lamentations* is a book of sad and mournful poetry about the destruction of Jerusalem. *Ecclesiastes* is a book of the teachings of King Solomon.

There are three historical books included in *K'tuvim: Daniel*, *Ezra and Nehemiah*, and *Chronicles I and II*. *Daniel* is the story of Daniel's triumph in the court of ancient Babylon. *Chronicles I and II* and *Ezra and Nehemiah* give us a history of the ancient land of Israel. *Chronicles* ends with the exile of the Jews to Babylonia. Ezra and Nehemiah were the men who led Israel when the Jews returned from Babylonia to Jerusalem. The book tells about the rebuilding of Jerusalem.

III. THE HAGIOGRAPHA —
(Sacred Writings)
a. The Three Poetical Books —
Sifre Emet (Books of Truth)
Psalms — Tehillim
Proverbs — Mishle
Job — Iyob
b. The Five Scrolls —
Song of Songs — Shir Hashirim
Ruth — Rut

Lamentations — Ekhah
Ecclesiastes — Kohelet
Esther — Esther
c. The Historical Books
Daniel — Daniel
Ezra — Ezra
Nehemiah — Nehemyah
Chronicles, I — Divre Hayamim, Aleph
Chronicles, II — Divre Hayamim, Bet

בְּרֵאשִׁית בָּרָא

WHEN GOD BEGAN CREATING

**BERESHIT
1:1–8**

¹When God began creating heaven and earth, ²The earth was a dark and shapeless mass, with a wind from God moving over the waters. ³Then God said, "Let there be light!" And there was light. ⁴God saw that the light was good, so God next divided the light from the darkness. ⁵God called the light "day" and the darkness "night." There was evening and there was morning, the first day. the h

---

3. THEN GOD SAID, "LET THERE BE LIGHT!"

וַיֹּאמֶר אֱלֹהִים יְהִי אוֹר

When a human being makes something, he needs tools and materials. The material is the substance you make something from, such as wood if you're making a carving. The tool is what you use, such as a carving knife. God, however, is not a human being and doesn't need tools and materials. God creates something simply by wanting it to exist. God has only to say "*Yehi!* Let there be!" and the something comes into existence. God does not need tools and does not need materials.

5. THERE WAS EVENING AND THERE WAS MORNING, THE FIRST DAY.

וַיְהִי־עֶרֶב וַיְהִי־בֹקֶר יוֹם אֶחָד

In the Torah, a full day begins with evening-time. Our Jewish holidays and festivals always start at evening-time. Shabbat starts on Friday evening and ends on Saturday evening. Yom Kippur starts on Kol Nidre eve and ends 24 hours later. All Jewish holidays start at evening-time.

⁶God said, "Let there be a dome to divide the waters." ⁷So God made the dome to separate the water which was below from the water above. And so it was. ⁸God called the dome, "sky." There was evening and there was morning, the second day.

---

7. SO GOD MADE THE DOME TO SEPARATE THE WATER.

וַיַּבְדֵּל בֵּין הַמַּיִם אֲשֶׁר מִתַּחַת לָרָקִיעַ וּבֵין הַמַּיִם אֲשֶׁר מֵעַל לָרָקִיעַ

In the Bible's description of the beginning of the world, there was at first a vast body of water. God created the "dome" of heaven—the sky (רָקִיעַ)—to divide the waters. After land is created, the waters below the רָקִיעַ will become seas, lakes, rivers, and springs; the waters above the רָקִיעַ become the rain and the dew.

8. GOD CALLED THE DOME "SKY."

וַיִּקְרָא אֱלֹהִים לָרָקִיעַ שָׁמָיִם

The Torah tells us that God named only six of his creations: night, darkness, sky, earth, sea, and man. Adam, God's only creature with intelligence, was given the task of naming all the other creatures and things.

Complete the Sentence

1. God called the light "___."
2. God called the _____ "night."
3. God said, "Let there be a _____."
4. This divided the _____.
5. It separated the water which was _____ from the water _____.
6. God called the dome, _____.

below, waters, dome, darkness, sky, above, day

Answer the Questions

1. Who is the creator?
2. What was the first thing God created?
3. What was the second thing God created?
4. Where was the dome?
5. What was the purpose of the dome?
6. What did God call the dome?
7. On what day of creation did God make the dome?

Ideas to Explore

1. Why do you think that God created light first?
2. What is the difference between making something out of some materials (like you make a kite out of papers, sticks, and string) and actually creating something?
3. Can anyone besides God *create* something?
4. Why did the earth need a sky?
5.. Could there be any earth if there were no separation between earth and sky?

הַטֶּבַע Our Environment

When the sky was created God separated the waters above (the water that gives us rain and dew) from the waters below (seas, lakes, rivers, and springs). No longer did water cover everything. The world became a place with air, as well as water. The air and water that God created were clean and beautiful. The environment He gave us was not polluted.

The word "environment" means everything around us, and the air and water make up most of our environment. So, doesn't it make sense to keep our air and water as clean as possible? You know, God's creating never really stopped. Wonders of nature take place every day. We can take part in creation by taking very good care of the gift of the world and by being very careful not to waste our natural resources.

Unfortunately, our environment is not nearly as clean and beautiful as it was when God gave it to us. We have not always used God's gifts wisely. Through accidents and carelessness, oil spills have ruined beaches, and waste products have polluted lakes and rivers. We have used up much of our natural resources. This is very sad because the words "life" and "environment" go together. Life must have a good, clean environment or it will disappear from the earth.

What Do You Think?

1. Write "Yes" or "No."
   a. People have taken good care of God's creation.
   b. My local neighborhood is working to keep our environment clean.
   c. We can win the war against the pollution of air and water.

2. What can *you* do to keep the environment clean?

3. Why do you think that people continue to waste our natural resources?

4. Do you think that some people hurt our environment "just for fun"?

5. People also destroy buildings or write on school walls "just for fun." When you look at the results of this kind of "fun," is it every funny?

יוֹם שְׁלִישִׁי – יוֹם רְבִיעִי
THE THIRD AND FOURTH DAY

**BERESHIT
1:9–19**

⁹God said, "Let the water under the sky be gathered into oceans so that the dry land may appear." ¹⁰God called the dry land "earth," and the gathering of water "seas." And God saw that this was good. ¹¹So God said, "Let the earth sprout grass, seed-bearing plants, fruit trees of every kind with seeds in the fruit, so that these seeds reproduce in turn." And so it was. ¹²The earth now brought forth grass, seed-bearing plants, fruit trees of every kind with seeds in the fruit, so that these seeds reproduce in turn. And God saw that all of this was good. ¹³There was evening and there was morning, the third full day.

11. "LET THE EARTH SPROUT GRASS."

תַּדְשֵׁא הָאָרֶץ דֶּשֶׁא עֵשֶׂב

Now, on the third day, God gathered the waters below the sky רָקִיעַ together so that dry land could appear—islands and continents. After the land rose up from the waters, God created growing things of all kinds—plants, trees, grass, herbs—all the many forms of vegetation that beautify the world.

12. AND GOD SAW THAT ALL THIS WAS GOOD.

וַיַּרְא אֱלֹהִים כִּי־טוֹב

God did not create the world by just adding different parts together. The Lord is a master builder and was following a carefully, organized plan. On each day of creation a different part of the plan was added to the world.

When all the parts of the plan were created they locked together like the pieces of a gigantic puzzle. The Torah gives us the details of God's plan of creation.

¹⁴Then God said, "Let there be lights in the sky to divide the day from the night. By their position shall the seasons, the days, and the years be recognized. ¹⁵Let them be up in the sky to give light down on the earth." And so it was, ¹⁶For God made two great lights: the larger one for the day and the smaller one for the night. God also created the stars. ¹⁷And God set them in the sky to give light on the earth, ¹⁸One during the day and the other through the night, and to separate the light from the darkness. And God saw that this was good. ¹⁹There was evening and there was morning, the fourth full day.

For example: When the light was created God said that "it was good". God did not say "it was good" when the dawn was created. The dawn was only a part of the creation of light.
The Lord was not satisfied with a tiny piece of the creation process. God was only satisfied when the complete phase was finished.

16. THE LARGER ONE FOR THE DAY
אֶת־הַמָּאוֹר הַגָּדֹל לְמֶמְשֶׁלֶת הַיּוֹם

The Torah says that the sun was created to give light to the earth. This is indeed what the sun does. It is most obvious during the day. But at night too and in many indirect ways, the sun is the source of our light here on earth.

For much of our light the two main fuels are, of course, coal and oil. However, both coal and oil in turn come from trees which lived long ago. Coal and oil have stored in them the energy to burn and give the light today exactly because the sun helped those trees to grow way back millions of years ago.

As the Torah says, the sun serves to give light to the earth—and it does so in many ways.

Match the Columns

1. God gathered the waters   day
2. God called the dry land   seas
3. God called the water   into oceans
4. God saw that this was   sprout grass
5. So God said, "Let the earth   good
6. The larger light shone during the   earth
7. The smaller light shone during the   night

Answer the Questions

1. What did God call the water?
2. What did God create after the seas and the earth?
3. What did God place in the sky on the fourth day?
4. What did the lights help to divide?
5. What do we call the larger light?
6. What do we call the smaller light?

Ideas to Explore

1. Do you think that God could have created the grass and trees on the first day? Why or why not?

2. Discuss how each of God's creations made possible the next step in creation (for example, dry land made a place for trees to grow).

3. God created the sun and moon to do many different things. How do they divide the day from the night?

4. How does the sun help us to tell the seasons?

5. How does the sun's position tell us when a year has passed?

בְּרָכוֹת BLESSINGS

God's world is a wonderful place in which to live. He peppered it with green valleys, ravishing rainbows, majestic mountains, bubbling brooks, marvelous animals and winds which whistle and sing through the trees. He perfumed His wonderful world with wondrous smelling flowers and plants.

We look at God's world with a great sense of wonder and joy.

The following blessings express our thanks for God's wonderful creations which involve the senses of sight, smell, and hearing.

(On hearing thunder.)

I praise God,	בָּרוּךְ אַתָּה,
Who is Lord,	יְיָ אֱלֹהֵינוּ,
And Ruler over all,	מֶלֶךְ הָעוֹלָם,
Whose strength and might fill the world..	שֶׁכֹּחוֹ וּגְבוּרָתוֹ מָלֵא עוֹלָם.

(On smelling fragrant plants.)

I praise God,	בָּרוּךְ אַתָּה,
Who is Lord,	יְיָ אֱלֹהֵינוּ,
And Ruler over all,	מֶלֶךְ הָעוֹלָם,
Who created fragrant spices.	בּוֹרֵא מִינֵי בְשָׂמִים.

I praise God,	בָּרוּךְ אַתָּה,
Who is Lord,	יְיָ אֱלֹהֵינוּ,
And King over all,	מֶלֶךְ הָעוֹלָם,
Who remembers the covenant,	זוֹכֵר הַבְּרִית
Ia faithful to the covenant,	וְנֶאֱמָן בִּבְרִיתוֹ
And keeps a promise.	וְקַיָּם בְּמַאֲמָרוֹ.

יוֹם חֲמִישִׁי

THE FIFTH DAY

BERESHIT 1:20–23

²⁰Then God said, "Let the waters be full of marine life, and let the skies be filled with birds." ²¹So God created the great sea monsters, and every kind of water creature, and every kind of bird. And God saw that this was good. ²²God blessed them all. "Grow in large numbers," God told them, "and fill the waters, and let the birds increase greatly on the land." ²³There was evening and there was morning, the fifth full day.

---

21. THE GREAT SEA MONSTERS.

הַתַּנִּינִם הַגְּדֹלִים

The Midrash tells us that the sea-monsters refer to the legendary Leviathan. Leviathan was the king of all the sea animals. So huge was Leviathan that he needed all the water from the river Jordan to quench his thirst. When he was hungry, a hot breath flowed from his nose which made the waters of the great sea boil.

The eyes of Leviathan emitted a light so brilliant that it blotted out the radiance of the sun.

22. GOD BLESSED THEM ALL.

וַיְבָרֶךְ אֹתָם אֱלֹהִים

On the fifth day of God's creation of the world, the first living creatures appear. God blessed the living creatures, They are part of a special plan. They are what they are not by accident, but because God wants them to be that way.

Pets

The Torah contains laws for the protection of animals—the laws of צַעַר בַּעֲלֵי חַיִּים The *tzaar baale chaim* laws protect animals against cruelty and give instructions for feeding and caring for our animal friends. If you have a pet, be sure to treat it as a friend—with plenty of tender, loving care.

Write an essay about pets in general, or about your own pet. In your essay, try to answer these questions.

1. Ever since Adam and Eve left the Garden of Eden, people have kept animals to work for them or as pets. What types of work have animals such as the ox, sheep, horse, and dog done?

2. What kinds of animals do people keep as pets?

3. Why do people keep animals as pets?

4. What kind of pet do you have or what kind of pet would you like to have?

5. How is your pet (or how would it be) special to you?

6. How do (or how would) you care for it? What special things do you do (or would you do) for your pet?

7. Why do you think we should take good care of pets?

8. If you saw someone hurting an animal, what would you do?

9. Do you know what the letters ASPCA stand for? What does the ASPCA do?

10. Can you think of any place in the United States where animals are still needed as man's helpers?

THE SIXTH DAY

יוֹם הַשִּׁשִּׁי

24Then God said, "Let there grow on the earth every kind of creature: cattle, reptiles, and wild animals of every kind." And so it was. 25For God made wild animals, cattle, and reptiles of every kind. And God saw that this was good. 26Then God said, "Let us make man similar to ourselves, to be the master of the fish of the sea and the birds of the sky, over the cattle and wildlife

---

26. LET US MAKE MAN SIMILAR TO OURSELVES.

נַעֲשֶׂה אָדָם בְּצַלְמֵנוּ

The Torah says that man was created in the image, or likeness, of God. This does not mean that human beings look like God or that God has an appearance that can be seen and duplicated. It means that human beings, both women and men, all have certain special powers and abilities. These are different from the powers and abilities of any other living creatures. On a much smaller scale they resemble God's special powers and abilities. Human beings can think, can invent and imagine things, have a sense of right and wrong. This is not true of any other living creature. All of these God-like abilities make human beings the high point of creation—the goal God was aiming at from the very beginning on the first day.

Because we have these special abilities, we are, in a way, God's partners in taking care of the world. He made the world and then gave it to us, but we have many responsibilities. For example, we must try to keep the world's air and water clean. We can either pollute the world or clean it up. By trying to make the world as clean and beautiful as it was when God created it, we are working with God to take care of the world.

of all the earth." ²⁷So God created man in God's own image. Male and female God created them. ²⁸And God blessed them, telling them, "Give birth to children. Fill the earth and become the masters of it by ruling over the fish of the seas, the birds of the skies, and all the living things that move on the earth." ²⁹Also, God said to them, "See, I have given you every seed-bearing plant on the earth, along with fruit trees, so that you will have all this food. ³¹Then God saw everything that was made, and it was all **excellent.** There was evening and there was morning, the sixth full day.

---

31. THEN GOD SAW EVERYTHING THAT HE HAD MADE, AND IT WAS ALL EXCELLENT.

וַיַּרְא אֱלֹהִים אֶת־כָּל־אֲשֶׁר עָשָׂה וְהִנֵּה־טוֹב מְאֹד

Now, on the sixth day, God creates the other animals. As the high point of the creation and the completion of a special plan, God creates man. Human beings are very different from all other living creatures. They have the ability to think, to choose, and to recognize the difference between right and wrong. God created the world and everything in it in order to make a place for man to live in. Since the creation of man is the final stage in God's plan, it comes at the end of the final day of creation. Now that creation is finished, God doesn't simply look at the world and say it is "good" (tov). Instead, God says that it is "excellent" (tov m'od).

Match the Columns

1. Let there grow on earth   that this was good
2. God made   wild animals, cattle, and reptiles
3. And God saw   every kind of creature
4. God said, "Let us make man   master over the other creatures
5. Man should be   similar to ourselves

Answer the Questions

1. What was the first thing God created on the sixth day?
2. What did God create next?
3. After God created man and woman, what did He do?
4. What was the blessing God gave them?
5. What did God give man to eat?

Ideas to Explore

1. Why did God create the birds, fish and animals before creating man?
2. Why did God make humans "the master of all living things"?
3. Was this a mistake?
4. Have "the masters of all living" things kept God's world in good condition?
5. How have they failed God?

You Are a Very Special Person

You are a very special person. You probably are the most special person that you know. Fill in the questionnaire and tell us something about yourself.

My name is:_____

My Hebrew name is: _____

My birthday is on:_____

I was born in: _____

My hair is: _____

My eyes are: _____

My hat size is: _____

My brain size is: _____

My favorite foods are:_____

The foods I love the least are: _____

I am very good at playing: _____

I am happy when: _____

I am sad when: _____

I like to spend my free time:_____

I would like to be good at:_____

The funniest thing I ever saw was: _____

The saddest thing I ever saw was: _____

When I was a baby I was special because:_____

Now I am special because: _____

When I grow up I plan to be special because: _____

What Do You Think?

1. Do you think that all people are created equal in the eyes of God?

2. Do you think that all people are born with equal abilities and equal chances to succeed in life? Discuss the difference between questions 1 and 2.

3. Do you think that everyone is treated equally in our society—blacks? Asians? Hispanics? women?

הַשַּׁבָּת

THE SABBATH

BERESHIT 2:1–4 ¹Now the heaven and earth were completed, along with everything in them. ²So having finished all the work by the seventh day, God stopped all further activity. ³And God blessed the seventh day, declaring it holy, because this was the day the Lord rested from the work of creation. ⁴Such is the story of the origin of the sky and the earth which the Lord God had made.

---

3. AND GOD BLESSED THE SEVENTH DAY, DECLARING IT HOLY.

וַיְבָרֶךְ אֱלֹהִים אֶת יוֹם הַשְּׁבִיעִי וַיְקַדֵּשׁ אוֹתוֹ

The six days of creation are over. God is very satisfied with the world and with the creatures which fill the world. God has completed the part of the plan that concerns matter—things you can see and touch. Now God is concerned with time. God separates the Sabbath from the other days of the week. The Sabbath is a time of complete rest—sanctified and holy. It is completely different from the ordinary days of the week, during which we are concerned with matter and material things—with our work and making things and other everyday concerns. Time now has meaning because it has been divided into separate parts—ordinary and holy. And now, at last, the work of creation is ended.

3. BECAUSE THIS WAS THE DAY WHEN THE LORD RESTED.

כִּי בוֹ שָׁבַת מִכָּל־מְלַאכְתּוֹ

In Hebrew the days of the week do not have special names such as Monday, Tuesday, and Wednesday, as in English. In Hebrew we call the days of the week יוֹם רִאשׁוֹן (first day), יוֹם שֵׁנִי (second day), and so on.

Only the seventh day, the Shabbat, deserved a special name. The name Shabbat comes from the Hebrew word שָׁבַת which means "to rest."

הַדְלָקַת הַנֵּרוֹת לְשַׁבָּת

Just as creation began with the joyous words "Let there be light," so does the beginning of the Sabbath begin with light. The parents welcome the Shabbat by performing the מִצְוָה of lighting the Shabbat candles. The brightly burning candles create an atmosphere of harmony, love, peace, and family togetherness.

I praise God,	בָּרוּךְ אַתָּה יְיָ,
Who is Lord, and Ruler over all,	אֱלֹהֵינוּ מֶלֶךְ הָעוֹלָם,
Who has made us holy with commandments,	אֲשֶׁר קִדְּשָׁנוּ בְּמִצְוֹתָיו
And commanded us	וְצִוָּנוּ
to kindle the Shabbat lights.	לְהַדְלִיק נֵר שֶׁל שַׁבָּת.

After the Shabbat candle-lighting, the parents express their love for the family by blessing the children.

To sons say.

God make you like	יְשִׂמְךָ אֱלֹהִים
Ephraim and Manasseh.	כְּאֶפְרַיִם וְכִמְנַשֶּׁה.

To daughters say:

God make you like Sarah,	יְשִׂמֵךְ אֱלֹהִים כְּשָׂרָה
Rebekah, Rachel and Leah.	רִבְקָה רָחֵל וְלֵאָה.

To sons and daughters:

May the Lord bless you and keep you;	יְבָרֶכְךָ יְיָ וְיִשְׁמְרֶךָ:
	יָאֵר יְיָ פָּנָיו אֵלֶיךָ וִיחֻנֶּךָ:
May the Lord turn towards you, and give you peace.	יִשָּׂא יְיָ פָּנָיו אֵלֶיךָ וְיָשֵׂם לְךָ שָׁלוֹם.

Answer " כֵּן " or " לֹא "

1. On the seventh day God still had more work to do. _____

2. On the seventh day God stopped all further activity. _____

3. God blessed the seventh day. _____

4. God declared the seventh day unholy. _____

5. On the seventh day God rested. _____

Answer the Questions

1. On what day of creation did God finish His work?

2. What did God do on the seventh day?

3. What did God bless?

4. Why was the seventh day different from the other days of creation?

Ideas to Explore

1. In the creation story, God separated light from darkness, water from water, water from dry land, even man from the other animals. What did God separate on the seventh day?

2. How are the six days of the week different from the seventh day for you?

3. Why do we rest on the Sabbath?

4. What are some of the special things about the Sabbath?

5. Do you think that the Sabbath is important to the Jewish people? Why?

The Sabbath

"*Challah. Barukh. Amen.*" Two-year-old David pointed excitedly at the table, all set for the Sabbath with gleaming china and silver, candles burning brightly, *challot* under the special *challah* cover, silver wine cup, and wine. Everything was ready for Father's return from synagogue. David made a dive for the *challah*.

"No, no, David," Mother stopped him gently. "Daddy will be home soon. He'll make *Kiddush* first and then . . ." At the word *Kiddush*, David ran to the bookshelf and grabbed a *siddur*. Returning to the dining room, he took his cup from the high-chair, opened the *siddur*, and said, "*Barukh. Amen.*" He smiled proudly.

"Very good, David," said Mother, giving him a hug.

Miriam stood in the doorway, lost in thought. Mechanically she folded and unfolded her arms. "Mom," she said suddenly, "why is David always so excited about the Sabbath? I mean, what can he understand about it? He's only a baby."

"Well, I guess he picks up things from us. And, anyway, who's to say that he doesn't have a נְשָׁמָה יְתֵרָה (*neshamah yeterah*) too?"

"A what?"

"A different soul, a special Sabbath spirit. You know what I mean?"

"Well, it does feel different around here on the Sabbath; that's true. The meal is special; there's *Kiddush*, the blessing over the *challah*, the Sabbath songs we sing. David gets to go to synagogue with all of us. And there's *Havdalah* at the end of the Sabbath, too."

"Yes, but don't forget the little things that add to the Sabbath spirit. There's no television blaring all day. Friends come and go all Sabbath afternoon. And, of course, since Daddy and I don't work, David sees much more of us. That helps to make the day special for him."

"For me too, Mom. When I think about it, on the Sabbath we're together more as a family. It's when we have our best talks. Like this one."

Miriam smiled. Mother smiled. And David happily proclaimed, "Sabbath."

THE GARDEN OF EDEN

גַּן־עֵדֶן

BERESHIT
2:8–25

[8]Then the Lord God planted a garden in Eden, in the East, and there the Lord put the newly created man. [9]Out of the ground God made beautiful trees to grow, which produced delicious fruit. God also put the Tree of Life at the center of the garden, along with the Tree of Knowledge, which gave knowledge of good and bad.

[15]The Lord God took the man and put him into the Garden of Eden, to cultivate it and to care for it. [16]But the Lord God instructed the man, saying, "You are free to eat of every tree of the garden, [17]Except of the Tree of Knowledge of good and bad, from which you must not eat. For on the day that you eat of it, you shall be doomed.

---

8. A GARDEN IN EDEN. גַּן־בְּעֵדֶן

Eden in Hebrew means "delight" or "happiness." The Garden of Eden had four rivers flowing through it. The garden was filled with tall trees, green grass, and beautiful flowers. The Garden of Eden was a delightful place in which to live, and Adam and Eve found much happiness there.

17. "EXCEPT OF THE TREE OF KNOWLEDGE OF GOOD AND BAD, FROM WHICH YOU MUST NOT EAT."

וּמֵעֵץ הַדַּעַת טוֹב וָרָע לֹא תֹאכַל מִמֶּנּוּ

God made a beautiful garden as a home for the first man and woman. They were free to use all the powers of their mind and body to enjoy the garden and its fruits, but they also had to exercise self-discipline. They had to restrain themselves by not eating from the fruit of the Tree of Knowledge.

[18]And the Lord God said, "It is not good for man to be alone. I shall make a companion to help him."
[21]So the Lord God put Adam into a deep sleep, and while the man slept, God took one of his ribs and closed up the place from which it was taken. [22]And the Lord God shaped the rib which was taken from man into a woman, and brought her to the man. [23] "This one is of my bone and flesh!" the man exclaimed. "She shall be called 'woman' because she was taken out of man." [25]Now, although the two of them were naked, they felt no shame.

---

22. AND THE LORD GOD SHAPED THE RIB WHICH WAS TAKEN FROM MAN INTO A WOMAN.

וַיִּבֶן יְהֹוָה אֱלֹהִים אֶת־הַצֵּלָע אֲשֶׁר־לָקַח מִן־הָאָדָם לְאִשָּׁה

Woman was not formed from the dust of the earth, she was formed from man's rib.

We are all born with twelve pairs of ribs which protect both sides of our body where the heart, liver, lungs, and many other vital life-giving organs are located. Without these ribs we could easily injure ourselves very badly and die.

God formed the woman from man's rib to symbolize the equal, side-by-side life partnership of man and woman.

As the ribs protect the vital life-giving organs from injury, so does the woman protect a family's well-being and vitality.

Complete the Sentence

1. God planted a garden in _____.
2. This land was located in the _____.
3. God put _____ in the garden.
4. Out of the ground grew beautiful _____.
5. The trees produced delicious _____.

fruit,man,trees,Eden,East

Answer the Questions

1. What tree was at the center of the Garden of Eden?
2. What other tree was alongside it?
3. Why was man put into the Garden of Eden?
4. From what tree were the man and woman not supposed to eat?
5. Did the man and woman wear clothes?

Ideas to Explore

1. Why do you think God created this special garden?
2. Why did he tell the man to take care of it?
3. What would happen to the man if he ate from the Tree of Knowledge?
4. Could the man eat from the Tree of Life?
5. What does this tell us about how long his life would have been in the Garden?
6. Why were the man and woman not ashamed of their nakedness?

Mitzvot מִצְווֹת

When God told Adam and Eve not to eat from the Tree of Knowledge, He was telling them to do His will, to do a מִצְוָה (mitzvah). The mitzvah was to listen to God by *not doing something;* it was a מִצְוַת לֹא־תַעֲשֶׂה (mitzvat lo taaseh). Many of our mitzvot, or commandments, are things that God tells us *to do,* מִצְוַת־עֲשֵׂה (mitzvat aseh)—like praying, for example.

If we want to live in a holy way, then we must do God's will by observing His commandments. At the same time that we do God's will, we also help ourselves because a mitzvah can make us happier or healthier or wiser or just better people.

There are 613 mitzvot in our Torah. There are mitzvot about holidays and ceremonies and many mitzvot about how to treat other people—like honoring your parents, sharing with others, helping people, being honest. When we do these mitzvot, we are doing something God wants us to do. Then we are good and we *feel good* too.

It is a mitzvah to pray. You know how it helps just to talk things over with your parents or friends. It helps even more to talk to God. Prayer is a mitzvah that makes us feel better inside ourselves.

You might not know it, but study is a mitzvah too, and a very important one. Parents and teachers used to give children honey cakes or drops of honey on the day their studies began. This showed the children that the study of the Torah is sweet and encouraged them to learn. Study is so important because it helps us to learn God's will. When we study the Torah, we learn about more mitzvot that we can do.

One mitzvah leads to another. For example, when you help someone, you may feel so good inside that before you know it, you find yourself helping someone else! Or when your family has a Passover seder, they may also do the mitzvah of inviting a guest to share the holiday with them.

The more mitzvot you do, the more you follow God's will, and you will be happier for it.

1. What is a mitzvah?

2. Why is it important to do mitzvot?

3. Can you think of a mitzvah that you did recently? How did you feel when you did it?

4. Do you think it's important to do a mitzvah willingly and wholeheartedly?

5. What if you did the mitzvah of giving charity, but you really didn't feel like doing it? Would it be better than not giving charity at all?

CAIN AND ABEL

קַיִן וְהֶבֶל

BERESHIT
4:1–12

¹Adam loved Eve his wife. She became pregnant after a while and gave birth to a son Cain, for she said, "I have gotten a child with God's help." ²Next she gave birth to his brother, Abel. Abel became a shepherd, and Cain became a farmer. ³After a time, Cain brought an offering to the Lord of grain from the fields. ⁴And Abel brought an offering of his **best** lambs. The Lord was pleased with Abel's offering. ⁵But God did not favor Cain's offering, and this made Cain very angry, and his face showed it.

4. AND ABEL BROUGHT AN OFFERING OF HIS BEST LAMBS.

וְהֶבֶל הֵבִיא גַם־הוּא מִבְּכֹרוֹת צֹאנוֹ

Abel's offering was from his "best" lambs. The word "best" does not appear in the description of Cain's offering. In other words, Cain was stingy in his approach to God. That is why his offering was rejected. Even though it was his own fault, he was jealous of Abel and blamed him. The same idea of blaming others appeared in the story of Adam and Eve. The Torah is telling us that to be mature (truly grown-up) you must accept responsibility for what you do.

⁸One day, Cain approached his brother and said, "Come, let's go out into the fields." And when they reached there, Cain attacked and killed Abel. ⁹Then the Lord said to Cain, "Where is your brother Abel?" To which Cain answered, "How should I know? Am I my brother's keeper!" ¹⁰And God said, "What have you done? Your brother's blood cries to Me from out of the ground. ¹¹Now you shall be cursed from that very ground which has opened up to receive your brother's blood spilled by your hand. ¹²When you now cultivate the ground, it shall no longer give you her crops. From now on, you will be a fugitive and a wanderer on the earth."

---

8. CAIN ATTACKED AND KILLED ABEL.

וַיָּקָם קַיִן אֶל־הֶבֶל אָחִיו וַיַּהַרְגֵהוּ

Cain's jealous hatred of Abel led to the first murder (which was also, in fact, the first death). Cain tries to deny any responsibility for the crime, but one cannot hide anything from God. God knows everything we do. He wanted Cain to admit his crime because then Cain would have to face the truth about himself. This would help him to become a better person.

12. FROM NOW ON, YOU WILL BE A FUGITIVE AND A WANDERER ON THE EARTH.

נָע וָנָד תִּהְיֶה בָאָרֶץ

God gave Cain two punishments. Cain would have no permanent home. He would have to wander from place to place looking for fertile, well-watered land.

Also, because he was a murderer, he would know no peace. People would chase after him all the days of his life.

Complete the Sentence

1. The first mother in the world was _____.
2. Adam and Eve's second child was _____.
3. _____ was a farmer.
4. Cain brought an offering of _____ to God.

Abel,grain,Eve,Cain

Answer the Questions

1. Who was Adam and Eve's first child?
2. What was his brother's name?
3. Who was the farmer?
4. Who was the shepherd?
5. What kinds of offerings did Cain and Abel bring?
6. Was God pleased with their offerings?

Ideas to Explore

1. Why do you think that Cain and Abel brought offerings to God?
2. Do we bring offerings to God today? What kind?
3. The Torah does not explain why God accepted only Abel's offering. Are lambs a better offering than grain, or is it the thought that counts? Can you find a clue in verses 3 and 4?
4. When your best friend has a birthday, do you buy him just anything? Why not?
5. How did Cain feel when God did not accept his offering? How did he show it?

The Family

Adam, Eve, Cain, and Abel were the very first family in the world. And how did the family come to be? The Torah tells us that "Adam loved Eve his wife." Every family starts with love. And love is what keeps a family together and makes it grow ever closer. Unfortunately, somewhere along the way, the members of the first family stopped loving each other enough. Maybe Adam and Eve quarreled because he blamed her for their having to leave the Garden of Eden. We know that Cain did not love Abel enough to share in his joy when God accepted Abel's offering. Instead, Cain became very jealous of his brother. That was an unhappy family.

When a family is guided by love, every family member is happy about the success and achievement of one of them. When one child gets an especially good report card, not only Mom and Dad, but also the other children are proud. And if one child disobeys his parents and makes a bad mistake, it's up to him or her to say, "I'm sorry I did that. I'll try to do better." And it's up to the rest of the family to help that child do better.

The members of a happy family share not only their possessions—their toys, clothes, and books—but also joys and sorrows, good times and bad. When there are problems—and there will *always* be problems—the family talks them out. They do their best to have שְׁלוֹם בַּיִת (shlom bayit), peace in the household.

It's not easy to keep *shlom bayit*. When problems come up, people lose their tempers, and sometimes *shlom bayit* flies right out the window! But it's certainly worthwhile to work at it because the warmth and closeness of a happy family is a precious gift. And years after the children have grown up and moved away, each family member is still a very special friend, someone you can always count on for advice, support, and love.

What Do You Think?

1. Is your family a close and happy one?

2. What can you do to keep *shlom bayit?*

3. If you have a brother or sister, do you share your things with them?

4. Do you try to obey your parents?

5. Does your family go on outings or take trips together? Do you enjoy spending time with your

נֹחַ אִישׁ צַדִּיק
NOAH WAS A RIGHTEOUS MAN

BERESHIT 6:9–22

9And this is the story of Noah's life: Noah was a really righteous man in his time. He followed God's way! 10And he had three sons: Shem, Ham, and Japhet. 11But the rest of the people on earth were outlaws and murderers. 12When God saw all of this evil, 13He said to Noah, "I have decided to end all of this. These violent people must go! 14So make yourself an Ark out of cypress wood. Seal it firmly with tar and then build into it many rooms. Build bottom, second, and third decks. 17 For I am about to bring a flood over the earth which will sweep away everything alive. 18Only to you, do I make My solemn promise, that you will enter the Ark

---

10. NOAH WAS A REALLY RIGHTEOUS MAN IN HIS TIME.
נֹחַ אִישׁ צַדִּיק תָּמִים הָיָה בְּדֹרֹתָיו

It is remarkable that Noah was able to remain a decent human being even though he lived in a wicked society. He was not influenced by the evil. The Bible calls Noah a *tzaddik*. He was a man of justice and righteousness compared to his neighbors, although perhaps he would not have measured up to the standards of a perfect society.

14. SO MAKE YOURSELF AN ARK OUT OF CYPRESS WOOD עֲשֵׂה לְךָ תֵּבַת עֲצֵי־גֹפֶר

The Rabbis say that Noah and his three sons worked for 120 years to complete the Ark. While the Ark was being built, Noah continued to warn the people that their wickedness would bring a great flood and would destroy them. For 120 years the wicked people laughed at Noah and continued to sin. Finally God sent the flood.

with your wife, your sons, and your son's wives. [19]And you shall take with you all living creatures, two of each kind, male and female, to keep them alive in the Ark. [20]Two of every kind, of bird and cattle and reptiles, shall come in with you in order to survive. [21]Take with you all the food that they and you will need." [22]Noah did everything exactly as God had instructed him.

[12]The rain fell on the earth for forty days and nights. [17]The flood now roared for forty days, covering the ground completely and raising the Ark high above the earth. [18]The waters rose higher and higher, but the Ark floated safely on the waters. [19]Finally, the waters covered even the highest mountains under the sky. [23]Everything on earth was wiped out. Only Noah and those who were with him in the Ark, survived.

---

23. EVERYTHING ON EARTH WAS WIPED OUT.

וַיִּמַח אֶת־כָּל־הַיְקוּם אֲשֶׁר עַל־פְּנֵי הָאֲדָמָה

Only those creatures who lived in the water were allowed to live. The water creatures had not been corrupted by the sins of the land creatures.

Complete the Sentence

1. Noah was a really _____ man.
2. Noah had _____ sons.
3. His sons were named Shem, Ham, and _____.
4. The other people on earth were outlaws and _____.
5. God decided to _____ all of this.

end, Japhet, murderers, righteous, three

Answer the Questions

1. When God decided to destroy the world, what did He tell Noah to do?
2. Why did Noah need an Ark?
3. Why did God bring the flood?
4. What did God promise Noah?
5. Who entered the Ark?

Ideas to Explore

1. Why do you think Noah was called a righteous man *in his time?* Do you think he would be considered righteous in our day too?
2. Can you imagine a world in which almost everyone was an outlaw or a murderer? Describe what life would be like. Do you see why God decided to destroy the world?
3. What do you think an Ark would be like? Describe it.
4. Why do you think God decided to destroy the world by flood rather than some other way?
5. Why do you think God decided to save some animals too?

צְדָקָה Tzedakah

"Noah was a really righteous man," a *tzaddik*. The Hebrew word for charity, *tzedakah*, comes from the same root צֶדֶק *(tzedek)*, meaning righteousness. That's because Jews never thought of giving *tzedakah* as something that you could choose to do or not to do. It was only *right*. What is right is holy too. So giving *tzedakah* is a great *mitzvah*. In fact, one of the rabbis quoted in the Talmud, Rav Assi, said, "Charity is equal to all *mitzvot*."

Tzedakah is an important part of Jewish life. People make donations to synagogue or temple to mark special occasions. They give extra *tzedakah* before Passover to help the needy buy *matzot* and other Passover foods. Jews keep *tzedakah* boxes in their homes, and many have made it a tradition to put money in the box before lighting Sabbath candles each Friday night. That's the sort of tradition that you could start in your home too. You can contribute to Israel, to many Jewish causes, and to other worthy causes. It just takes a few cents of your allowance or birthday or Hanukkah money to earn an important *mitzvah*. It doesn't really matter how much you give, but *how* you give is important.

The great scholar Maimonides put the Jewish ideas about how to give charity into a simple code called the "Ladder of *Tzedakah*." It tells us the eight degrees of giving charity. It explains the best ways to give *tzedakah*.

Eight degrees of charity starting with the most important.

1. Helping someone to help himself.
2. Giving anonymously to an unknown person.
3. Giving anonymously to a person you know is in need.
4. Giving without knowing who will get the gift.
5. Giving without being asked.
6. Giving after being asked.
7. Giving less than one can afford, but giving willingly.
8. Giving unwillingly.

What Do You Think?

1. When was the last time you gave *tzedakah*? To whom or to what organization did you give?
2. Do you think you should give *tzedakah* to anyone who asks or do you think you should be careful to find out what purpose your money will be used for?
3. Give an example of each of Maimonides' eight degrees of *tzedakah*.

עַל הָרֵי אֲרָרָט
ON THE MOUNTAINS OF ARARAT

BERESHIT
8:4–21

⁴At the end of this time, the Ark came to rest on the mountains of Ararat, on the 17th day of the seventh month. ⁵The waters continued to go down until the tenth month. ⁶On the 10th day of the eleventh month, Noah opened a porthole, ⁷And he released a raven that flew back and forth until the earth was dry. ⁸Next, he released a dove to see whether that bird could find dry ground. ⁹But the dove could find no spot to rest, because there was still water on the ground. So Noah reached out his hand and brought the dove back into the Ark. ¹⁰Noah waited another seven days, and once again he released the dove. ¹¹Toward evening of that day, the dove returned to him with a fresh olive-leaf in her beak. Then Noah knew that the water was almost completely gone. ¹²He waited another week and released the dove again. But this third time she did not return.

---

11. WITH A FRESH OLIVE-LEAF IN HER BEAK.

וְהִנֵּה עֲלֵה־זַיִת טָרָף בְּפִיהָ

The green olive-leaf was proof that the flood waters had gone down to the point that plant life could grow.

¹⁸So Noah came out with all of his family. ¹⁹And with them there came out from the Ark all the other creatures. ²⁰Then Noah built an altar to the Lord, and he sacrificed some of the clean animals and birds. ²¹And God was pleased with Noah's sacrifices. He said to Himself, "Never again will I doom the world because of man. ¹²"And this," God continued, "is 9:12-17 the sign of the promise that I am setting up between Me and you for all time to come. ¹³I have put My rainbow in the clouds as the sign of the covenant between Me and the earth. ¹⁶For I will see the rainbow in the clouds and I will remember this eternal promise." ¹⁷"That," God said to Noah, "will be the sign of the promise which I have set between Me and every living creature on the earth."

---

13. I HAVE PUT MY RAINBOW IN THE CLOUDS
אֶת־קַשְׁתִּי נָתַתִּי בֶּעָנָן

If people in the future ever become frightened by dark clouds and threatening rain clouds, the rainbow will assure them that there is no need to fear another terrible flood.

16. FOR I WILL SEE THE RAINBOW IN THE CLOUDS AND I WILL REMEMBER THIS ETERNAL PROMISE.

וְהָיְתָה הַקֶּשֶׁת בֶּעָנָן וּרְאִיתִיהָ לִזְכֹּר בְּרִית עוֹלָם

The rainbow is a sign of God's covenant. God's loving-kindness and mercy toward the people in the world.

There is a special prayer which is recited when we see the rainbow. "I praise God, who is Ruler and Lord over all, who remembers the covenant, is faithful to the covenant, and keeps the promise."

Answer " כֵּן " or " לֹא "

1. The Ark came to rest in a valley.
2. At first Noah sent a raven from the Ark.
3. Next, he sent the raven back again.
4. The dove returned because there was still water on the ground.
5. Noah waited three weeks before releasing the dove again.

Answer the Questions

1. Was God pleased with Noah's offering?
2. What did God promise?
3. What happened seven days after Noah released the dove for the first time?
4. What was in the dove's beak?
5. What did this tell Noah?
6. How long did Noah wait before sending the dove out again?
7. What happened then?

Ideas to Explore

1. Noah thanked God by offering God something of value—animals. How do we thank God today?
2. Do you think that prayer has the same value as sacrifice? Which do you think is a better way to thank God?
3. In this passage, did God promise never to destroy man again?
4. What do you think God meant by the last part of His promise? Explain.

הַבְּרִית

Covenant

It's just after a heavy rainstorm, and the sun, in all its brilliance, breaks through the clouds. Suddenly a dazzling arc of colors appears in the sky—everything from vivid red to royal purple. This beautifully colored sight is created when white light from the sun hits the raindrops which are still in the air after a storm. Although the rainbow is really a circle, the bottom half is hidden from our eyes, lying below the horizon.

The shimmering brightness of the rainbow is certainly a reassuring symbol that the rain is over and once again God has kept His covenant—"that life shall never again be cut down by the floodwaters."

That was the first covenant made with a human. Later, God would make a covenant with Avraham and with others of our forefathers.

But exactly what is a covenant? It is an agreement or a promise, often depending on certain conditions. Sometimes a covenant is spelled out, and sometimes it is just understood. For example, when people live together as a family, they have an unwritten, perhaps unspoken, covenant with each other. Each family member promises to care for the others. They may not discuss it, but it's still understood. A simpler kind of covenant might be between a school crossing guard and the children. The guard promises to watch for cars and control the traffic, while the children promise to obey the guard.

Every time you see a rainbow, you should remember how God has honored that first covenant. Each one of us should do his or her best to honor the covenants that we make in our lives.

What Do You Think?

1. What is a covenant?
2. Give an example of a covenant.
3. Tell about a covenant that you have made.
4. Did you keep your end of the agreement?
5. Did the other person keep his or her end?

מִגְדַּל בָּבֶל

THE TOWER OF BABEL

BERESHIT 11:1-9

¹At that time, all humans spoke the same language and had the same ideas. ²Mankind began to spread eastward, where they discovered a valley in the land of Shinar, and they settled there. ³After a while they said to each other, "Come, let us make bricks and bake them solid. ⁴With these, let us build a great city and a ziggurat to reach into the sky! It shall be a monument for us and it will unite us." ⁵The Lord saw the city and the ziggurat which the men had built. ⁶He said, "If this is how they have begun to act, while they are one people with one language for all, think of what else they may yet do! Soon nothing will be too hard for them. ⁷Let me therefore go down and confuse their language so that they will no longer understand each other!" ⁸Then the Lord scattered them across the earth, and the city was not finished. ⁹That is why it came to be called Babel, because the Lord confused them by giving them many languages, as they scattered across the earth.

3. LET US MAKE BRICKS AND BAKE THEM SOLID

הָבָה נִלְבְּנָה לְבֵנִים וְנִשְׂרְפָה לִשְׂרֵפָה

Our Rabbis tell us that the people of Babel cared more for their bricks than for the lives of their builders. When a brick fell and killed someone, they became angry about the brick and the time lost. They were not concerned about the person who was killed or who was hurt.

The name of the tower was called Babel. The word *bavel* means "confused." That is exactly what God did to these cruel people. He confused their language so they could not understand each other.

Match the Columns

1. In those days everyone spoke   ziggurat (temple tower)
2. The people settled in a   one language
3. They wanted to build a   confusing their language
4. They built the tower with   valley
5. God punished them by   bricks

Answer the Questions

1. Where did the people settle?
2. What did they decide to do?
3. Why did the people decide to do this?
4. Did they want to build a monument to God?
5. Do you think that it would be possible to build a ziggurat (temple-tower) that would reach the sky?

Ideas to Explore

1. Do you think it was wrong for the people to want to build such a tower?
2. When the people of Babel were building their tower, what do you think was more important to them—
   a. finishing the tower no matter what (even if people were hurt or killed)?
   b. caring for one another and remembering the importance of every person and animal on earth?
3. God confused their speech. What do you think this means?
4. Why couldn't the people continue to work on the tower after God confused their speech?
5. What do you think about God's punishment?
6. Did you ever wonder how people came to live in different lands and speak different languages? How does the story of the Tower of Babel explain this?

The Use of Language

The people who built the Tower of Babel may have been able to say "Pass me a brick" or "Let's have a hammer up here, willya?" but they weren't really using their language to communicate. They didn't use their language to try to understand each other and help each other or even to work together on something of value. To them, language was just a tool for barking orders that would help them finish their "skyscraper," their ziggurat. This is why God chose to punish them by confusing their language. Not only did they have to stop work on the tower, but this punishment also made them stop and think about the way that they were using language.

After all, language is one of the greatest gifts that God has given us. Just imagine what the world would be like without it! No books, or movies, or television, of course. How difficult it would be to make anything that takes the work of more than one person!

Since we do have language, it's important that we use it the right way—for kindness and truth, for helping people and making them happy. Before we speak we should always ask ourselves: Am I saying something that will hurt someone's feelings? Am I using clean language?

What Do You Think?

1. How did the people who built the Tower of Babel use language?

2. How should language be used?

3. Why would it be difficult for two or more people to work together without language?

4. Could we learn from each other, and would there be schools, if there were no such thing as language?

5. Can you think of a time that you used language badly and hurt someone else's feelings?

6. How did you feel afterwards? What did you do?

7. Are you careful to think before you speak?

Language can be used for good and for evil. Look at the following situations in which language is being used. What kind of language would you use to answer?

You tell your friend a secret and he promises to keep it. Now your friend turns around and blabs your secret. What do you say?

_____

_____

_____

_____

_____

A friend says, "Give me some money and I'll be your best friend." What do you answer?

_____

_____

_____

_____

Your friend wants you to help play a trick on the teacher. He promises you that no one will ever find out about it. What do you say?

_____

_____

_____

_____

TEACHER

לֶךְ־לְךָ מֵאַרְצְךָ LEAVE YOUR COUNTRY

¹Now the Lord said to Avram, "Leave your country, your people, and your father's house, and go to a land where I will guide you. ²There I shall make you the father of a great nation. I will bless you and make your name famous, and you shall be a blessing. ³I shall bless those who bless you and curse those who curse you, and through you shall the whole world be blessed." ⁴So Avram migrated from Haran as the Lord had instructed him to do, and Lot went with him. At that time, Avram was 75 years old. ⁵He took his wife Sarai, his nephew Lot, and all that Avram owned. Together they made their way from Haran to Canaan.

1. LEAVE YOUR COUNTRY, YOUR PEOPLE, AND YOUR FATHER'S HOUSE, AND GO TO A LAND WHERE I WILL GUIDE YOU.

לֶךְ־לְךָ מֵאַרְצְךָ וּמִמּוֹלַדְתְּךָ וּמִבֵּית אָבִיךָ אֶל־הָאָרֶץ אֲשֶׁר אַרְאֶךָּ

It is hard to leave your country, where you have your roots and speak the language. It is even harder to leave your people—your friends and relatives. It is most difficult to leave your father's house, where you were brought up and where the rest of your family lives. For Avram, there was no hesitation or questioning. At God's command, Avram left his country, his people, and his father's house.

2. I WILL BLESS YOU AND MAKE YOUR NAME FAMOUS, AND YOU SHALL BE A BLESSING.

וַאֲבָרֶכְךָ וַאֲגַדְּלָה שְׁמֶךָ וֶהְיֵה בְּרָכָה

Wherever Avram would go, and his descendants after him, they would bring feelings of love and mercy for other human beings. These would be "blessings" which would improve mankind. Avram and his descendants would help to lead people away from the evils of idol-worshipping religions.

Match the Columns

1. God promised to make   wife
   Avram the
2. Avram went to   Haran
3. Lot was Avram's   nephew
4. Sarai was Avram's   Canaan
5. Avram migrated from   father of a great nation

Answer the Questions

1. What did God ask Avram to do?
2. Where did God send Avram?
3. What did God promise Avram?
4. Whom did God promise to bless because of Avram?
5. What would happen to those who cursed Avram?
6. Who left Haran with Avram?
7. How old was Avram when he left Haran?

Ideas to Explore

1. God said to Avram, "You shall be a blessing." What do you think this means?
2. How would you feel if you were asked to leave your home and you were not even told where to go?
3. How do you think Avram felt?

אַבְרָם יָשַׁב בְּאֶרֶץ־כְּנָעַן
AVRAM REMAINED IN THE LAND OF CANAAN

BERESHIT
13:1–12

¹From Egypt they returned north to the Negev—Avram, his wife, and Lot, and all that they owned. ²For Avram was very rich in livestock, and silver and gold.

⁵Lot, too, was wealthy. He had sheep and cattle, and tents. ⁶But the land was not enough for pasture if they were to remain together. ⁷Fights had broken out between the herdsmen of Avram and those of Lot. ⁸So Avram discussed the situation with Lot. "We must end this fighting between us," said Avram. "We are, after all, of the same family. ⁹And there is certainly a large area of land around us. Choose, therefore, whichever land you wish, and we will separate. If you go to the left, then I

---

5. LOT, TOO, WAS WEALTHY. HE HAD SHEEP
AND CATTLE

וְגַם לְלוֹט הַהֹלֵךְ אֶת־אַבְרָם הָיָה צֹאן־וּבָקָר

Lot's wealth came because he was very close to Avram. God blesses all those who are close to righteous people.

9. CHOOSE, THEREFORE, WHICHEVER LAND
YOU WISH, AND WE WILL SEPARATE.

הִפָּרֶד נָא מֵעָלָי

The families of Avram and Lot lived peacefully together. All went well until the shepherds began to quarrel about the grass and the water. Avram was a man of peace and hated quarrels, so he said to his nephew, Lot, "Choose, therefore, whichever land you wish, and we will separate." This was noble and generous of Avram, for he was the eldest and could have claimed the first choice. Avram went out of his way just to preserve peace and keep Lot as his friend.

shall go to the right; or if you go to the right, then I shall go to the left." ¹⁰Lot looked out over the countryside and his eyes set on the plains of the Jordan River. It was like a richly watered garden, similar to the fertile land around Zoar, in Egypt. ¹¹So Lot chose for himself the plain of the Jordan to the east, and he separated from Avram. ¹²Avram remained in the land of Canaan while Lot lived among the cities of the Jordan plain, pitching his tents near Sodom.

---

10. LOT LOOKED OUT OVER THE COUNTRYSIDE AND HIS EYES SET ON THE PLAINS OF THE JORDAN RIVER.

וַיִּשָּׂא־לוֹט אֶת־עֵינָיו וַיַּרְא אֶת־כָּל־כִּכַּר הַיַּרְדֵּן

Lot looked over the land and decided that he would settle on the great plain of the Jordan River. This land was unusually beautiful, and the soil was very fertile with plenty of water. The flowers and vegetables that grew there were large and perfect.

Lot was aware that the cities of Sodom and Gomorrah were also on the plain of Jordan. He knew that the people in those two cities were evil and worshipped idols. Yet Lot chose to live among the idol-worshippers of Sodom. The grass for his sheep and the rich crops were more important than the kind of neighbors he would have to live with.

The Jordan River rises in the mountains of Lebanon and Syria and flows into Lake Kinneret. From there, the rapidly falling waters of the river flow into the Jordan Valley and then end up in the Dead Sea, one of the hottest places on earth. For most of its 135-mile length, it is impossible to navigate the Jordan by boat. Today the Jordan River is the boundary between the State of Israel and the Kingdom of Jordan. Two bridges cross the river and connect the two countries.

Complete the Sentence

1. Avram, Sarai, and Lot returned _____ to the Negev.
2. Avram was very rich in _____, and silver, and gold.
3. _____ had sheep, and cattle, and tents.
4. They didn't have enough land for _____.
5. The herdsmen of Lot and the herdsmen of _____ were fighting.

Avram, Lot, north, pasture, livestock

Answer the Questions

1. What was Avram's solution to the fight over pasture land?
2. What portion of land did Lot choose for himself?
3. Near what city did Lot live?

Ideas to Explore

1. Do you think that Avram was wise to leave Haran as God had told him to? Did he prosper?
2. From the way Avram chose to settle his dispute with Lot, what kind of man would you say Avram was?
3. What kind of land did Lot choose for himself? What does this tell you about Lot?
4. What have you heard about the city of Sodom where Lot pitched his tents?
5. Did Lot's choice show that he valued money more than morals? Discuss.
6. Was it possible for Avram and Lot to share the same land?

Laws For The Needy

When the shepherds of Avram and Lot quarreled, Avram gave Lot his pick of the land. Avram wanted to provide Lot with the means to make a living. Among no people of old was there so much concern shown for the livelihood of those in want as in Israel. In the ancient Hebrew state, the poor were assured of a living by the rights which the Bible gave them in the harvest. These rights were five in number:

1. The poor had the right to any crops that grew in the corners of the field—*Peah* (Corner).
2. The poor had the right to crops dropped on the ground when the corn was being picked—*Leket* (Gathering).
3. The poor had the right to isolated grapes on the vine,—*Olelot* (Young Clusters).
4. The poor had the right to grapes that were not perfect—*Olelot* (Young Clusters).
5. The poor had the right to sheaves that were forgotten by the farmer—*Shikchah* (Forgetfulness).

All these parts of the harvest belonged to the poor. The farmer was not allowed to gather them, and all needy people—the poor, the widow, the orphan, and the stranger (whether Jew or non-Jew)—were entitled to them.

There was also a special poor tax, known as מַעֲשֵׂר עָנִי, Poor Tithe. Twice in seven years the Jewish farmer had to set aside one tenth of this harvest and take it to a special storehouse in the district where Poor Tithe was kept for distribution to the needy.

אֵלֹנֵי מַמְרֵא

THE OAKS OF MAMRE

[14]After Lot had gone, the Almighty said to Avram, "Raise your eyes and look as far as you can to the North, South, East, and the West. [15]For all of the land that you can see, I give to you and to your descendants after you. [16]As for your descendants, them will I make as countless as the grains of sand! [17]Take yourself a tour through the length and width of the land and you will see what I am giving you."

[18]Then Avram moved his tents to the oaks of Mamre at Hebron, and he built an altar there to the Lord.

---

14. AFTER LOT HAD GONE, THE ALMIGHTY SAID TO AVRAM.

וַיהוָה אָמַר אֶל־אַבְרָם אַחֲרֵי הִפָּרֶד־לוֹט מֵעִמּוֹ

God knew that blessing Avram while Lot was still with him would make Lot grow even more jealous of his uncle's wealth. Therefore, God waited till Lot had gone on his way to Sodom and then blessed Avram.

15. FOR ALL OF THE LAND THAT YOU CAN SEE, I GIVE TO YOU AND TO YOUR DESCENDANTS.

כִּי אֶת־כָּל־הָאָרֶץ אֲשֶׁר־אַתָּה רֹאֶה לְךָ אֶתְּנֶנָּה וּלְזַרְעֲךָ עַד עוֹלָם

This blessing was given to each of the three Patriarchs, Avraham, Yitzchak, and Yaakov.

16. AS COUNTLESS AS THE GRAINS OF SAND.

כַּעֲפַר הָאָרֶץ

Try counting the grains of sand in a teaspoon. How many grains of sand are there on a small beach? in the world? They are beyond number and countless.

Symbols And Trophies

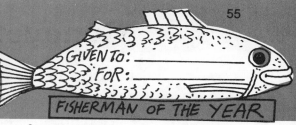

The Torah not only teaches us great ideas, but it does so in beautiful language, simple language that uses symbols to help us understand ideas. In this story God promises to make Avram's descendants as many as the grains of sand. In other places in the Torah, God promises to make the Jews as numerous as the stars in the sky. In the story of Noach, God uses the dove and the rainbow to illustrate the ideas of peace and happiness.

Suppose you were asked to award and design trophies for deserving people. You could use symbols to stand for the special qualities of those people. Design these symbolic trophies and list the reasons you would present them to certain people.

Neighbor of the Year Given to For	Friend of the Year Given to For
Politician of the Year Given to For	Relative of the Year Given to For

Complete the Sentence

1. After Lot had gone, the Lord spoke to _____.
2. God told Avram to look in every _____.
3. God promised the land to Avram and his _____.
4. Avram's descendants would be _____.
5. There would be as many Jews as grains of _____.

sand, direction, Avram, countless, descendants

Answer the Questions

1. How much land did God promise to give Avram?
2. Did he promise it to Avram only?
3. How many descendants did God say Avram would have?
4. Where did Avram move his tents?
5. How did Avram show his thanks to the Lord?

Ideas to Explore

1. God made this promise to Avram just after Lot left. What had Avram given to Lot?
2. Why do you think God gave this land to Avram?
3. God promised the land to Avram and his descendants. Does that mean that we have the earliest claim to the Land of Israel? Does it give us the rights to the State of Israel today?
4. When Avram moved his tents, he built an altar to the Lord. What can we learn from this?

Making Decisions

Avram gave Lot a choice and he made the decision to live on the Plain of Jordan. Lot chose to live with good land and bad people. Do you think he made the right choice?

Making a decision means picking and choosing. The things you choose from are called choices. Decisions may be made from many, few, or just two choices. Sometimes, when one choice seems very right to you, you may feel that you have no choice. But it is important to learn to make decisions, to take a stand. And of course you should try to make your decisions good ones.

Think about decisions you make every day: what to eat for breakfast, what clothes to wear, what games to play, or who will be on your team. Your parents make decisions, too. They decide where you and the family will live, the food to buy, and the synagogue they will attend.

Name one decision you made at home. _____

What were your choices? _____

Why did you make that special choice? _____

Do you think that you made the right decision? Why or why not? _____

_____

Name one decision you made at school. _____

What were your choices? _____

Why did you make that special choice? _____

Do you think that you made the right decision? Why or why not? _____

_____

Name one decision you made at play. _____

What were your choices? _____

Why did you make that special choice? _____

Do you think that you made the right decision? Why or why not? _____

_____

וְקָרָאת שְׁמוֹ יִשְׁמָעֵאל
YOU WILL CALL HIM YISHMAEL

¹Sarai and Avram had no children. But Sarai had a maidservant, an Egyptian girl named Hagar. ²And Sarai said to Avram, "Since the Almighty has not given you children through me, I give you now my maidservant. Marry her and let her children be in place of mine." Avram agreed. ³This happened ten years after they had arrived in Canaan.

⁴After Avram married Hagar, she became pregnant. ⁵So Sarai complained to Avram, "It's all your fault! Ever since Hagar has been pregnant, she has despised me. And to think that it was I who gave her to you! May the Lord judge between me and you." ⁶And Avram answered Sarai, "Look, the maid is yours. You may do with her as you see fit." So Sarai punished her and she ran away.

⁷Afterward, an angel of the Lord found Hagar at a desert spring on the road to Shur. The angel asked her, "Hagar, maid of Sarai, where have you come from and where are you going?" ⁸She replied, "I am running away from my

---

2. I GIVE YOU NOW MY MAIDSERVANT.

בֹּא־נָא אֶל־שִׁפְחָתִי

Sarai loved Avram and wanted so much for him to be happy that she said to him, "Avram, take my maidservant, Hagar, as your wife. Perhaps she will have the child we want so badly." Sarai loved Avram so much that she was willing to share his love with another woman.

mistress." ⁹But the angel of the Almighty said to her, "You must return to your mistress and do whatever she orders." ¹⁰"In return for your obedience," the angel added, "I will make your descendants into a very large nation." ¹¹And the angel of the Almighty spoke further to her, "You are now pregnant and you shall give birth to a son. You will call him Yishmael, for God has heard your complaints. ¹²He shall be a wild donkey, his hand against everyone, and everyone's hand against him, always in opposition to his fellow men."
¹⁵Then Hagar gave birth to Avram's son, whom Avram named Yishmael. ¹⁶Avram was 86 years old at Yishmael's birth.

---

10. I WILL MAKE YOUR DESCENDANTS INTO A VERY LARGE NATION. הַרְבָּה אַרְבֶּה אֶת־זַרְעֵךְ

Two great nations are descended from Avram, the Jews and the Arabs. The Jews are the descendants of Avram's second son, Yitzchak, whom we will learn about in another unit. The Arabs are descendants of Avram's son by Hagar, Yishmael.

11. YOU WILL CALL HIM YISHMAEL. וְקָרָאת שְׁמוֹ יִשְׁמָעֵאל

Yishmael in Hebrew can be divided into two words: יִשְׁמַע meaning "will hear," and אֵל, meaning "God." Together, "God will hear." God heard Hagar's prayers and answered them.

12. HE SHALL BE A WILD DONKEY, HIS HAND AGAINST EVERYONE. וְהוּא יִהְיֶה פֶּרֶא אָדָם יָדוֹ בַכֹּל

Yishmael, Avram's first-born son, did not inherit his father's estate but led a nomad's life in the desert. Yishmael was a wild donkey of a man (Hebrew פֶּרֶא אָדָם). A man or a tribe that cannot fit itself to civilized life is like a wild donkey. Yishmael did not live in the midst of his brethren, but "his hand is against everyone" and he was constantly at war with them.

Answer the Questions

1. Did Sarai and Avram have any children at this time?

2. Where was Hagar from?

3. Why did Sarai give Hagar to Avram to marry?

4. How many years had Avram and Sarai been living in Canaan?

5. What happened between Sarai and Hagar when Hagar became pregnant?

6. What was Avram's solution to the problem?

Complete the Sentence

1. Hagar ran away because Sarai _____ her.

2. An angel found Hagar at a _____ _____ on the road to Shur.

3. The angel told Hagar to _____ to Sarai.

4. The angel promised Hagar that her descendants would be a large _____.

5. The angel said that Yishmael would be a _____.

punished, return, wild donkey, nation, desert spring

Ideas to Explore

1. What is a concubine? Does she have the same position as a wife? Was Hagar a wife or a concubine?

2. Do you think that Sarai did the right thing in giving Hagar to Avram to marry? Was her act a selfish or an unselfish one?

3. Why do you think that Hagar might have "despised" Sarai, or been disrespectful to her, after Hagar became pregnant?

4. If you were Avram, what would you have done about Hagar's behavior?

5. If you were Sarai, would you have punished Hagar? Why or why not?

Consultations And Decisions

Before punishing Hagar, Sarai consulted with her husband Avram. Sarai wanted another opinion before taking action.

Simple decisions such as choosing an ice cream flavor or a TV program do not require consultation or special advice. But sometimes we are faced with problems that need a more expert opinion. Then it is a good idea to ask and consult.

Whom would you consult in these situations?

Choose the person from the "line-up" that you would consult in each of the following situations.

Your bicycle was stolen. You would call a _____

You are not feeling well and your nose bleeds.

You will call the _____

You want to join the temple choir.

You will call the _____ .

You wish to discuss a new project for the temple youth group.

You will call the _____

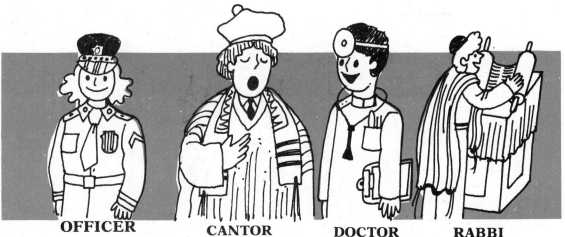

OFFICER   CANTOR   DOCTOR   RABBI

וְאֶעֶשְׂךָ לְגוֹי גָּדוֹל

I SHALL MAKE YOU THE FATHER OF A GREAT NATION

BERESHIT 17:1–17

[1]When Avram was 99 years old, the Lord appeared to him and said, "I am God Almighty. Follow my ways and have full faith in Me. [2]I will make a Covenant between us, and I will make you into a large nation." [3]Avram now bowed to the ground as God spoke further to him. [4]"And this is My Covenant with you: You shall be the father of nations. [5]Nor shall your name any longer be called 'Avram.' From now on, your name shall be 'Avraham,' meaning that I make you 'the father of great nations.' [6]I will give you many descendants who will, in turn, make up nations. Rulers, too, will there be among your descendants. [7]And I will keep this Covenant between us, and with your descendants after you for all of the generations ahead, to be your and their God forever. [8]I give you and your descendants this land of Canaan in which you now live, as an ever-lasting possession."

---

2. I WILL MAKE A COVENANT BETWEEN US.
וְאֶתְּנָה בְרִיתִי בֵּינִי וּבֵינֶךָ

Avram refused to believe in gods who acted like human beings. He believed in one God who required people to live a life of justice, freedom, and brotherhood.

God was pleased with Avram and made a Covenant with him promising that his descendants would become a great nation.

5. FROM NOW ON, YOUR NAME SHALL BE "AVRAHAM."
וְהָיָה שִׁמְךָ אַבְרָהָם

God honors Avram by adding the letter ה to his name, thus changing it to Avraham, meaning "the father of great nations."

¹¹You shall circumcise the flesh of your foreskin; and that shall be the sign of your loyalty to this Covenant. ¹²Every male among you is to be circumcised on the eighth day after birth."

¹⁵Then God said to Avraham, "As for Sarai, your wife, call her no longer 'Sarai.' Let her name now be 'Sarah.' ¹⁶I will bless her and give you a son with her; I will make her a mother of nations. Rulers of people will be her descendants." ¹⁷Avraham bowed to the ground in tribute to God.

---

12. EVERY MALE AMONG YOU IS TO BE CIRCUMCISED ON THE EIGHTH DAY AFTER BIRTH.

וּבֶן־שְׁמֹנַת יָמִים יִמּוֹל לָכֶם כָּל־זָכָר

On the eighth day after birth, a baby boy undergoes circumcision (בְּרִית מִילָה). The person who performs this religious rite is called a מוֹהֵל. At the ceremony the boy is also given his Hebrew name.

A girl receives her name in the temple when her parents are called to the Torah on the Shabbat following the birth.

15. LET HER NAME NOW BE "SARAH." כִּי שָׂרָה שְׁמָה

God added the letter ה to Avram's name and changed it to Avraham. Now God adds the letter ה to Sarai's name and renames her Sarah. The letter ה is sometimes used as a shorthand for the name of God.

At first her name was Sarai, meaning "my princess." Sarai was a princess only to the Patriarch, Avraham. Now, because of her goodness and many מִצְווֹת, God renames her "Sarah," meaning "princess to all." Sarah was now elevated to a princess to all and a special blessing to the whole world.

64

Answer " כֵּן " or " לֹא "

1. Avram was ninety-eight years old when God made a Covenant with him. _____

2. God promised to make Avram into a large nation. _____

3. God promised to make Avram the father of nations. _____

4. God did not change Avram's name. _____

5. God said that Avram's descendants would be slaves. _____

Answer the Questions

1. For how long did God promise to keep the Covenant with Avraham and his descendants?

2. What land did God promise to give us?

3. What is the sign of our loyalty to the Covenant?

4. On what day after birth should each Jewish male be circumcised?

5. What was Sarai's name changed to?

6. What did God promise Sarah?

Ideas to Explore

1. What is a Covenant?

2. What do we mean when we call the Jews "the chosen people"? What does this idea have to do with the Covenant?

3. Why do you think that God might have chosen circumcision as a sign of loyalty to the Covenant?

4. Why do you think that God changed Avraham's and Sarah's names?

5. Since God had already promised to make Avraham a father of nations, why did God later promise to make Sarah a mother of nations? Was this just a case of repeating the same thing for emphasis?

אֶרֶץ חָלָב וּדְבַשׁ
Flowing With Milk And Honey

The Torah tells us that long, long ago the Land of Canaan (now the State of Israel) was "a land flowing with milk and honey," a rich, sweet land. Ancient Israel was a fertile land, kept green by a nation of dedicated farmers.

But because Israel was such a rich land, other nations were always fighting for it and trying to conquer it.

About 2,000 years ago, the Jews were driven from their beloved land. In the course of time, the land became a useless desert.

But the Jews do not give up easily. Many years later, in 1890, the חֲלוּצִים (pioneers) started returning to Israel. They built dams, dug wells, drained the water from swamps—and miraculously the land began to live again.

Today the State of Israel is a beautiful, fertile place. Once again golden oranges hang from the trees and huge clusters of grapes hang from the vines. The Israelis are now more skilled as farmers than ever before. The Israeli government sends farm experts to poorer countries to live with the people and teach them better ways to farm. Thus Israel shares with its fellow nations and helps make the world a better, more beautiful place in which to live.

וְהִנֵּה בֵן לְשָׂרָה אִשְׁתֶּךָ
SARAH SHALL HAVE A SON

¹Again the Almighty appeared to Avraham when he was living in the oak country of Mamre. This happened one hot summer's day while Avraham was sitting at the entrance to his tent. ²Looking up, he saw three men standing at a short distance from him. He rushed forward to welcome them. ³"My lords," Avraham said, "please go no further, for I am your servant. ⁴Stop with us a while and rest yourselves in the shade of the tree, while we get you some water to bathe your feet. ⁵And we will prepare for you a bit of food to refresh you. Then you can continue on your journey." They answered, "Very well, do as you have said."

⁶Then Avraham hurried into the tent and instructed Sarah, "Quick! Get out our best flour and bake some round wafers." ⁷Next, Avraham ran to his herd, took a

---

1. WHILE AVRAHAM WAS SITTING AT THE ENTRANCE TO HIS TENT

וְהוּא יֹשֵׁב פֶּתַח־הָאֹהֶל

Wherever Avraham lived, his home was open to strangers. He never failed to show hospitality and kindness to those in need.

Avraham, the great Hebrew leader, showed his concern for humanity and his love of God by practicing hospitality. הַכְנָסַת אוֹרְחִים (welcoming guests) is a great מִצְוָה.

Our Sages tell us that when Avraham lived in Mamre, he planted a lovely garden and placed around it four gates. One gate faced north, one south, one east, and one west. A weary traveler coming from any direction would find an open door into the cool garden, where he could rest, eat, and drink.

fat calf, and gave it to a servant-boy to prepare. [8]Then he took some yogurt and milk, and the calf which had been prepared by now. He set all this before the guests, and waited on them under the tree as they ate.

[9]"Where is your wife Sarah?" they asked him. "There, inside the tent," he replied. [10]Then one of them said, "When I come back next year at this season, you and your wife Sarah shall have a son!" Meanwhile, Sarah was listening inside the tent. [11]Now, Avraham and Sarah were old people. And Sarah was long past the time when she might give birth to a child. [12]So Sarah laughed to herself, saying, "A woman of my age have a child? And with a husband as old as mine?" [13]Then the Lord said to Avraham, "Why did Sarah laugh at the possibility of having a child? [14]Is anything impossible for the Lord? Next year, at this season, Sarah will indeed have a son!"

---

7. NEXT, AVRAHAM RAN TO HIS HERD, TOOK A FAT CALF, AND GAVE IT TO A SERVANT-BOY TO PREPARE.

וְאֶל־הַבָּקָר רָץ אַבְרָהָם וַיִּקַּח בֶּן־בָּקָר רַךְ וָטוֹב וַיִּתֵּן אֶל־הַנַּעַר וַיְמַהֵר לַעֲשׂוֹת אֹתוֹ

The boy was Avraham's son Yishmael, whom he was trying to teach the מִצְוָה of הַכְנָסַת אוֹרְחִים

8. HE SET ALL THIS BEFORE THE GUESTS.

וַיִּתֵּן לִפְנֵיהֶם

Avraham provided his guests with a meal of the best he could offer: the best flour, calf's meat, yogurt and milk. On Avraham's orders, Sarah made the guests cakes of the finest flour meal. These were a thin flat cake which required very little baking, similar to the מַצּוֹת baked by the Israelites when they left Egypt.

Complete the Sentence

1. Avraham was living in the oak country of _____.
2. One summer's day Avraham saw _____ men approaching his tent.
3. Avraham invited them to _____ in the shade.
4. He brought the guests _____ to bathe their feet.
5. He offered them _____.

three, food, Mamre, water, rest,

Answer the Questions

1. What did Avraham ask Sarah to bake?
2. What did he give to a servant-boy to prepare?
3. What did Avraham serve his guests by himself?
4. What did one guest promise Sarah?
5. Why did Sarah laugh?
6. What did God promise?

Ideas to Explore

1. Some say that Avraham's guests were really angels. Do you agree? Why or why not?
2. Avraham always helped strangers and travelers. What type of welcome did he give them? What can we learn from the way Avraham treated his guests?
3. If you were Sarah, would you have laughed at the idea of an old woman having a child?

Generous Gestures

Generosity means giving and sharing freely with others, without expecting any return. There are lots of times in your life when you have the chance to be generous. For example, you could be generous by cleaning your room without your mother asking you to do it.

How was Avraham generous to his three visitors?

_____

_____

_____

List the ways you could be generous to others and others could be generous to you.

WAYS TO BE GENEROUS TO MY FAMILY:

_____

_____

_____

_____

WAYS TO BE GENEROUS TO MY FRIENDS:

_____

_____

_____

_____

WAYS TO BE GENEROUS TO MY COMMUNITY:

_____

_____

_____

_____

_____

_____

זַעֲקַת סְדֹם וַעֲמֹרָה כִּי־רָבָּה
THE WRONGDOINGS OF SODOM AND GOMORRAH CRY OUT AGAINST THEM

BERESHIT 18:20–22 20So God said to Avraham, "The wrong-doings of Sodom and Gomorrah cry out against them. Their sins are very great. 21I am going down there now to decide what to do."

22The men who had visited with Avraham were moving on toward Sodom,

BERESHIT 19:1–29 1In the evening, the two messengers arrived in Sodom as Lot was relaxing at the city gate. When he saw the visitors, Lot got up and welcomed them. 2He said, "Please, sirs, come to our home for the night. Then, tomorrow morning, you can move on again." But they said, "No, we will spend the night right here in the public square." 3But he urged them so strongly that they agreed. They came home with him. He prepared a meal for them, complete with fresh-baked wafers, which they ate.

---

22. THE MEN WHO HAD VISITED WITH AVRAHAM WERE MOVING ON TOWARD SODOM.

וַיִּפְנוּ מִשָּׁם הָאֲנָשִׁים וַיֵּלְכוּ סְדֹמָה

Three angels in the form of men were sent to Avraham. One was sent to notify Avraham that Sarah would have a son. The second angel was sent to destroy Sodom. The third angel was sent to save Lot and his family. Each angel had only one task to perform.

¹⁵When dawn broke, the messengers hurried Lot, saying, "Take your wife and two daughters so that you may escape the destruction of this city." ¹⁶But Lot delayed. So the visitors took hold of his hand and the hands of his wife and two daughters, and rushed them out of the city, for the Lord was kind to them. ¹⁷When they had brought them outside the city, they told Lot, "Run for your life! Don't look behind you, nor stop anywhere on the plain!" ²³As Lot reached Zoar, the sun was rising. ²⁴In the meanwhile, the Almighty rained down sulphurous fire from above, on Sodom and Gomorrah. ²⁵The Almighty destroyed those cities and their surrounding region, eliminating all of their inhabitants, along with all of the vegetation. ²⁶And Lot's wife, who was following behind him, dared to look back, and she turned into a pillar of salt.

²⁹So it was that God remembered Avraham and rescued Lot from the catastrophe which destroyed the cities.

23. AS LOT REACHED ZOAR, THE SUN WAS RISING.
הַשֶּׁמֶשׁ יָצָא עַל־הָאָרֶץ וְלוֹט בָּא צֹעֲרָה

Our wise Sages tell us that God chose a special day on which to destroy the wicked city of Sodom. It was the sixteenth of the month Nissan, the day when both the sun and the moon could be seen together.

"If the moon alone were out," said God, "those who worship the sun would say that the sun could have saved them had it been here. If the sun alone were in the sky, the moon-worshippers would cry that the moon could have saved them. Therefore, let both sun and moon be here together when the city is destroyed. Let the people know that the sun and the moon are not gods but creations of the one true God—the only God they should worship."

Match the Columns

1. Two messengers came to   Lot
2. The messengers came in the   home
3. They were welcomed by   Sodom
4. Lot invited them   public square
5. They wished to sleep in the   evening

Answer the Questions

1. Why was God considering destroying Sodom and Gomorrah?
2. Did Avraham know someone who lived in Sodom? Who?
3. Did the messengers agree to go to Lot's home? Why?
4. What did the messengers tell Lot? Did he listen immediately?
5. How did the messengers help Lot and his family?
6. When they were outside the city, what did the messengers warn Lot and his family not to do?
7. Who did not listen, and what happened to that person?

What Do You Think?

1. Why do you think that Avraham asked God to save Sodom and Gomorrah?
2. From whom do you think Lot learned to be hospitable?
3. Why do you think Lot failed to leave Sodom immediately?

   Why do you think that Lot and his family were not supposed to look back?

הַכְנָסַת אוֹרְחִים
Welcoming A New Neighbor

Lot welcomes the three strangers by offering them food and a place to sleep. Lot makes them feel at home by preparing the food himself and by serving them personally.

Imagine someone your age has moved into a house nearby. How would you go about welcoming the newcomer into the neighborhood and making him or her feel at home?

One day the two of you start talking about your temple. Your new friend starts asking questions.

Fill in the balloons to show what you would say to each other.

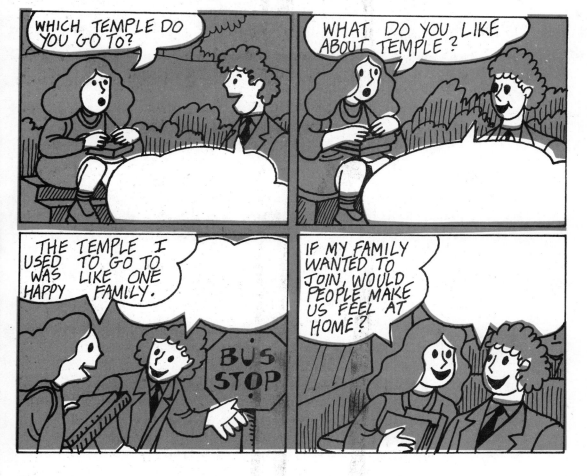

וַיהוָה פָּקַד אֶת־שָׂרָה

AT LAST GOD REMEMBERED SARAH

BERESHIT 21:1–8 [1]At last God remembered Sarah and fulfilled the promise to her. [2]Sarah became pregnant and gave birth to a son. She and Avraham now had a child in their old age, as God had promised. [3]And Avraham named their son, Yitzchak. [4]Avraham circumcised Yitzchak when he was eight days old, as God had instructed him. [5]Now, Avraham was 100 years old when his son Yitzchak was born.

[6]"God has brought me laughter," Sarah said. "Everyone who hears about this will laugh at me." [7]She also said, "Who would ever have said to Avraham that Sarah might nurse children! Yet I gave birth to his son in his old age."

[8]The child grew and was weaned.

---

1. AT LAST GOD REMEMBERED SARAH. וַיהוָה פָּקַד אֶת־שָׂרָה

This section comes after the preceding one to teach that they who pray on behalf of others, as Avraham did for the people of Sodom, will have their own wishes granted by God.

3. YITZCHAK. יִצְחָק

The name Yitzchak comes from the word צָחַק, which means "to laugh." The Torah says that Sarah laughed when she heard God say she would have a child despite her advanced age.

4. AVRAHAM CIRCUMCISED YITZCHAK.

וַיָּמָל אַבְרָהָם אֶת־יִצְחָק

Eight days after a boy is born we perform a ceremony called בְּרִית מִילָה. This ceremony makes every boy a בֶּן בְּרִית ("son of the covenant"). Judaism sees God and man as partners and co-workers. This idea is expressed in the idea of a covenant–a בְּרִית. A covenant is a relationship in which two parties freely accept certain obligations toward each other.

And that is why we, the children of Israel, are sometime refered to as בְּנֵי בְּרִית ("children of the covenant").

Answer the Questions

1. What promise to Sarah did God fulfill?
2. What was Sarah's son named?
3. What did his name mean?
4. When did Avraham circumcise the child?
5. How old was Avraham when Yitzchak was born?

Ideas to Explore

1. By giving Sarah a son, God was really fulfilling two promises to her. What were these two promises?
2. Would you consider the birth of Yitzchak a miracle?

What Do You Think?

God is also called "Ruler of the universe."
What does this name tell us about what we think of God?

Another name is "Our Divine Parent."
What does this name tell us about what we think of God?

Another name for God is "Lord."
What does this name tell us about how we think of God?

Another name for God is "Almighty."
What two words do you see in this name?
What does this name tell us about how we think of God?

וַיֵּלְכוּ שְׁנֵיהֶם יַחְדָּו

AND THEY WALKED FURTHER TOGETHER

BERESHIT 22:1–14

¹After some time had passed, God put Avraham to the test. God called to him, "Avraham!" And Avraham answered, "I am ready." ²And God said, "Take your very beloved son Yitzchak, and go to the land of Moriah, where you shall offer him as a sacrifice on one of the hills that I will point out to you." ³Early next morning, Avraham saddled his donkey and took two of his servant-boys along with his son Yitzchak. They cut wood for the burnt-offering and started out for the place to where God had told them to go. ⁴On the third day of their journey, Avraham looked up and saw the place in the distance. ⁵Then Avraham said to his servants, "You stay here with the donkey while the boy and I go on to the place. We will worship there and come back to you."

---

1. I AM READY. הִנֵּנִי

Avraham was always ready to receive and obey God's command, whether it was to leave his father's home or to sacrifice his own son.

2. TAKE YOUR VERY BELOVED SON YITZCHAK, AND GO TO THE LAND OF MORIAH, WHERE YOU SHALL OFFER HIM AS A SACRIFICE.

קַח־נָא אֶת־בִּנְךָ אֶת־יְחִידְךָ אֲשֶׁר־אָהַבְתָּ אֶת־יִצְחָק

Avraham could scarcely believe his ears. Why had God asked him to make such a sacrifice? But Avraham, in his great wisdom, was a man of complete faith. His loyalty to God was to become an example to his descendants, who would be just as loyal, even if it meant losing their homes, their livelihood, and sadly, sometimes their lives.

⁶Avraham put the wood for the burnt-offering on Yitz-chak's back, while he himself carried the flint for the fire and a knife. ⁷Then Yitzchak said to his father, "We have the wood and the flint for the fire, but where is the sheep for the offering?" ⁸"God will provide that, my son," Avraham answered. And they walked further together. ⁹When they reached the place where God had told Avraham to go, he built an altar there and piled the wood on it. Then he bound his son Yitzchak and laid him on top of the wood. ¹⁰Now Avraham picked up the knife with which to sacrifice his son. ¹¹But at that very moment, an angel of the Almighty called to him from heaven, "Avraham! Avraham!" ¹²Avraham stopped to listen. The angel spoke again, "Do not lay a hand against the boy. I know now that you have complete faith in God, for you have not held back from Me even your beloved son." ¹³Then Avraham saw a ram caught in a bush by its horns. So Avraham took the ram and offered it as a sacrifice instead of his son. ¹⁴Avraham named the place "AdonaiYireh," which later became a saying: "On God's mountain God has seen and provided."

---

13. SO AVRAHAM TOOK THE RAM AND OFFERED IT AS A SACRIFICE INSTEAD OF HIS SON.

וַיִּקַּח אֶת־הָאַיִל וַיַּעֲלֵהוּ לְעֹלָה תַּחַת בְּנוֹ

The sounding of the Shofar, or ram's horn, on Rosh Hashanah serves as a reminder of the horns of the ram that was sacrificed by Avraham in place of Yitzchak.

The practice of sacrificing animals is as old as humankind. The Hebrew word for sacrifice is קָרְבָּן, which comes from the verb קָרוֹב, meaning "to come near." The purpose of sacrifices was to bring the Jews close to God.

When the people came to the Holy Temple in Jerusalem to sacrifice animals, they also prayed to God and heard the beautiful music of the Levites and the singing of the Psalms.

Since the destruction of the Second Temple in 70 C.E., we no longer have animal sacrifices. In their place we now substitute תְּפִלָּה (prayer).

78

Answer " כֵּן " or " לֹא "

1. When God called Avraham to test him, Avraham answered, "I'm not ready." _____
2. God told Avraham to take Yitzchak to Moriah and sacrifice him on a hill. _____
3. Avraham took Yitzchak, two servants, and a horse on the journey. _____
4. They traveled for ten days. _____
5. Avraham and Yitzchak completed the journey alone. _____

Answer the Questions

1. Who carried the wood for the burnt-offering?
2. What did Yitzchak ask?
3. After Avraham built an altar and piled the wood on it, what did he do?
4. What happened just as Avraham was about to sacrifice his son?
5. Did Avraham pass his test?
6. What did he sacrifice instead of Yitzchak?

Ideas to Explore

1. In asking Avraham to sacrifice Yitzchak, why did God call him "your very beloved son"? Did that make Avraham's test even harder?
2. Why do you think that Avraham preferred to face his test without others watching?
3. Avraham told his servants, "We will worship there and come back to you." Do you think that he believed his own words?
4. Do you think that Avraham really intended to kill his own son? Do you think that he expected God to stop him?
5. What would you have done in Avraham's place?

כַּבֵּד אֶת אָבִיךָ וְאֶת אִמֶּךָ

Honor Thy Father And Thy Mother

Avraham had complete faith in the goodness of God. With great sorrow he took his beloved son to be sacrificed. Yitzchak had complete faith in his father's love. He honored his father and obeyed his wishes to the point of willingly offering himself as a sacrifice.

Just about the first words every child learns to say are "Mommy" and "Daddy." When frightened by something, a child cries out, "Mommy! I want Mommy!" or "Daddy! Daddy!" Even when children grow older, Mom and Dad are the first ones they turn to for help and love.

Jews have always been known as a people who respect and love their families. Not just Mom and Dad but brothers, sisters, aunts, uncles, and cousins. Members of Jewish families help each other out when there is a problem of any kind, or if money is needed for something.

You are a very important member of your family. So, do your best in school. Be kind and polite at home. Help Mom and Dad in any way you can to show them how glad and grateful you are for their loving care. By doing all these things, you will help make your whole family a happy one. You will also be living up to the Fifth Commandment, which says: "Honor Thy Father and Thy Mother."

What Do You Think?

1. Have you ever been asked to do something that didn't make sense to you?

2. Who asked you to do it?

3. Did you do it?

4. Have your parents ever asked you to do something that didn't make sense to you?

5. What did you say?

תְּנוּ לִי אֲחֻזַּת־קֶבֶר עִמָּכֶם

I NEED A BURIAL PLACE FOR MY WIFE

BERESHIT 23:1–20 ¹Sarah lived 127 years. ²She died in Kiryath-arba, which is Hebron, in the land of Canaan. ³Then Avraham got up from mourning his dead wife and he spoke to the men of Cheth, ⁴"I am an immigrant among you, having come from another country. Now I need a burial place for my wife. Would you sell me a piece of land for that purpose?" ⁵"Hear us, my lord," the Chethites replied. ⁶"You are a mighty prince among us. Choose for yourself whichever burial ground you wish, and no one will refuse you." ⁷Then Avraham bowed before the men of

2. SHE DIED IN KIRYATH–ARBA, WHICH IS HEBRON, IN THE LAND OF CANAAN.

וַתָּמָת שָׂרָה בְּקִרְיַת אַרְבַּע הִוא חֶבְרוֹן בְּאֶרֶץ כְּנָעַן

Hebron (which means "association, group") is a city in Israel 19 miles southwest of Jerusalem. It is situated in a valley and is surrounded by olive groves and by vineyards.

It was in the city of Hebron that Avraham bought the family grave, the Cave of Machpelah. A walled enclosure about 200 by 100 feet has been built on the traditional site of the Cave of Machpelah. The construction is similar to that of the Temple area in Jerusalem. Within the wall is a Moslem mosque. Inside the mosque is the Cave of Machpelah, which contains the graves of the three Patriarchs and their wives, except for Rachel.

2. KIRYATH–ARBA. בְּקִרְיַת אַרְבַּע

This name, which means "city of the four," is said to refer to the four couples who are buried there: Adam and Eve, Avraham and Sarah, Yitzchak and Rivkah, Yaakov and Leah.

Cheth. [8]He said to them, "If you are willing, then I would ask you to speak for me to Efron, the son of Zochar. [9]Let him sell me the Cave of Machpelah which he owns. It is at the edge of his property. Let him sell it to me in your presence, at its full price, as a burial place."

[10]Efron the Chethite, who was sitting among them, now spoke before his fellow citizens, [11]"No, my lord, listen to me. I will give you the field, along with the cave, at no charge to you. I will give it to you as a gift right now in the presence of my people." [12]Again Avraham bowed before the local citizens. [13]He spoke to Efron as all of them listened, "If you are really willing, let me make you a proposal. I will pay you for the land. Please accept the money; and I will bury my dead there." [14]Efron answered Avraham, [15]"My lord, please listen to me. The land is worth 400 shekels of silver, but what does that money matter to you and me? Go now and bury your dead one." [16]So Avraham paid Efron the amount which he mentioned in the presence of the Chethites. Avraham paid 400 shekels of silver, which was the form of currency.

[17]So Efron's land in Machpelah, facing Mamre, which included the cave and all the surrounding land, became [18]the property of Avraham, in the presence of all the Chethites. [19]Then Avraham buried his wife in the Cave of Machpelah, facing Mamre, which is Hebron, in the land of Canaan. [20]In this way did the field, with its cave, pass from the Chethites to Avraham as a burial place.

---

7. THEN AVRAHAM BOWED BEFORE THE MEN OF CHETH.

וַיִּשְׁתַּחוּ לְעַם־הָאָרֶץ לִבְנֵי חֵת

Bowing was part of ancient Eastern custom. It was a sign of respect for authority. Here, Avraham was also thanking them for their kindness in offering him burial ground.

Complete the Sentence

1. Sarah lived to be _____.
2. Sarah died in Kiryath-arba, which is_____.
3. Hebron is in the land of _____.
4. Avraham asked the men of _____ to sell him land for a burial place.
5. The Chethites told Avraham to take any_____he wished.

burial ground, Hebron, 127, Cheth, Canaan

Answer the Questions

1. What land did Avraham want to buy?
2. Whom did it belong to?
3. Was Avraham offered the land for free?
4. How much did Avraham pay for the land?
5. Where did Avraham bury Sarah?

Ideas to Explore

1. Why do you think the Chethites offered Avraham land for free? Was the offer a sincere one?
2. Do you think that the conversation between Avraham and Efron might have been just a polite, ancient form of bargaining?
3. Does the price of 400 shekels of silver sound pretty expensive to you?
4. Why do you suppose that Avraham insisted on paying for the Cave of Machpelah?
5. Notice that Avraham paid in the presence of witnesses. Why do you think he did so?

Eshet Chayal　אֵשֶׁת חַיִל

This hymn is taken from the Book of Proverbs (31:10–31) and is chanted when returning home from the synagogue on Friday night.

It is written in the form of an alphabetical acrostic, with the first letter of each verse representing another letter of the Hebrew alphabet. Thus, the first word is *eshet*, the first word of the second verse is *batach*, etc.

To this day the term אֵשֶׁת חַיִל, a "woman of valor," is used by Jews to describe the finest type of Jewish woman and helpmate. When we say of a woman that "she was a true *eshet chayil*," we mean that she was a devoted wife and mother who observed Jewish law and tradition to the letter. She was the type of woman who deserves the praise our Sages gave to the Matriarchs Sarah and Rivkah: "As long as Sarah lived a cloud of light hung over her tent. When she died the light departed. When Rivkah came, it returned. As long as Sarah lived, her doors were open wide. When she died they were closed. When Rivkah came they were opened again. As long as Sarah lived there was a blessing on her dough, and the lamp used to burn from the evening of the Sabbath until the evening of the following Sabbath. When she died these stopped. When Rivkah came they returned."

A woman of valor who can find her?
Her worth is far above rubies.

אֵשֶׁת חַיִל מִי יִמְצָא,
וְרָחֹק מִפְּנִינִים מִכְרָהּ:

The heart of her husband trusts her;
and he has no lack of gain.

בָּטַח בָּהּ לֵב בַּעְלָהּ,
וְשָׁלָל לֹא יֶחְסָר:

She does him good and not harm,
all the days of her life.

גְּמָלַתְהוּ טוֹב וְלֹא־רָע,
כֹּל יְמֵי חַיֶּיהָ:

Give her the fruit of her hands;
and let her deeds be praised.

תְּנוּ־לָהּ מִפְּרִי יָדֶיהָ,
וִיהַלְלוּהָ בַשְּׁעָרִים מַעֲשֶׂיהָ:

וְלָקַחְתָּ אִשָּׁה לִבְנִי לְיִצְחָק

AND GET A WIFE FOR MY SON YITZCHOK

¹Avraham was now a very old man. The Almighty had blessed him in every way. ²So Avraham spoke to his trusted servant who was in charge of his household, saying, "Make me a solemn promise. ³Swear by the Almighty God of heaven and earth, that you will not take a wife for my son from among the Canaanites. ⁴Go, instead, to my home country, to my family there, and get a wife for my son Yitzchak.

¹⁰The servant took ten of his master's camels and loaded them with valuable gifts and he set out on his journey to Aram-naharayim, where Nachor lived. ¹¹When he arrived there, he made the camels kneel down near a well outside the city. It was evening, and the women were coming out to draw water. ¹²"Almighty, God of my master

---

1. THE ALMIGHTY HAD BLESSED HIM IN EVERY WAY.
וַיהוָה בֵּרַךְ אֶת־אַבְרָהָם בַּכֹּל

The numerical value of the Hebrew word בַּכֹּל ("in every way") is 52, equal to the numerical value of the word בֵּן ("son"); in other words, God had blessed Avraham "in every way" by giving him the son he had wanted—Yitzchak.

2. SO AVRAHAM SPOKE TO HIS TRUSTED SERVANT.
וַיֹּאמֶר אַבְרָהָם אֶל־עַבְדּוֹ זְקַן בֵּיתוֹ

The name of the servant is not mentioned here. Later on the servant is identified as Eliezer. As chief of the servants in the household of Avraham, Eliezer supervised the activities of all the other servants. Avraham would have wanted to go on this mission himself, but he was too old for such a long journey.

Avraham," he prayed, "be kind to my master and make me successful today.

¹⁵He had hardly finished speaking when Rivkah arrived with a jug on her shoulder. She was the daughter of Bethuel son of Nachor and his wife Milcah. ¹⁶Rivkah, a beautiful girl, went down to the well and filled her jug. ¹⁷Rushing over to her, the servant said, "Please let me have some water from your jug." ¹⁸"Drink, sir," she replied, and quickly lowered the jug for him to drink. ¹⁹After she had let him drink, she said, "I will draw some water for your camels, too, until they have enough to drink."

²⁰Quickly emptying her jug into the trough, she ran back to the well and drew water for all the camels.

²¹All this while, the man watched her and wondered whether the Almighty had already made his mission a success.

---

19. I WILL DRAW SOME WATER FOR YOUR CAMELS, TOO. גַּם לִגְמַלֶּיךָ אֶשְׁאָב

Rivkah worked a long time drawing water for all the camels. It was hard work but she asked no reward. She performed the task out of mercy for the camels. Eliezer realized that he had found a fitting wife for Yitzchak, and offered her the presents he had brought with him for the bride-to-be.

Match the Columns

1. Yitzchak's father was   Nachor
2. Bethuel's father was   Yitzchak
3. Nachor's wife was   Rivkah
4. Bethuel's daughter was   Avraham
5. Rivkah was chosen to marry   Milcah

Answer the Questions

1. How many camels were in Eliezer's caravan?
2. Did Eliezer ask Rivkah to water the camels?
3. Was it difficult to water the camels?
4. Why did Rivkah volunteer to water the camels?
5. Why was Eliezer pleased when Rivkah volunteered to water the camels?

What Do You Think?

1. Why do you think Avraham wanted a wife for Yitzchak from his own family and not from the Canaanites?

2. Would you say that Avraham was a man of tremendous faith? Why?

3. Why do you think Avraham's servant took along so many valuable gifts?

4. Was the test that Avraham's servant created a good one?

5. What qualities of a good wife or a good person did it test for?

עֲשֶׂרֶת הַדִּבְּרוֹת לִבְהֵמוֹת
Ten Commandments for Animals

Both Avraham's servant and the young Rivkah showed concern for his camels—making sure to give them water. So we see that Jews have a long tradition of being kind to animals. Not only are we forbidden to be cruel to animals, but we have laws to protect them—sort of a Ten Commandments for the Good of Animals.

1. An animal that falls down must be raised with the same care as if it were a human being.
2. While an animal works to tread out corn, it may not be muzzled, but must be allowed to eat from the grain.
3. Animals of different species, like an ox and an ass, must not be yoked together for work. Since they have different strengths, it is cruel to force them to work together under one yoke.
4. Animals must be allowed to rest from working on the Sabbath, just as the owner has to rest.
5. We are not allowed to sit down to a meal before feeding our animals or pets.
6. We are not allowed to give an animal a heavier load than it can bear.
7. We are not allowed to hit an animal if it is not necessary.
8. We may not buy any animal or bird unless we can provide enough food for it.
9. Killing animals or birds for sport is forbidden.
10. In slaughtering animals or birds for food, we must try not to cause unnecessary pain. The Jewish laws of *Shechitah* are designed to keep animals from suffering when meat is prepared for eating.

There are also other Jewish laws that protect animals from cruelty. If you take care to follow them, you will be certain to treat animals kindly and to become a kinder person yourself.

לֹא אֹכַל עַד אִם־דִּבַּרְתִּי דְּבָרָי

I WILL NOT EAT BEFORE I TELL YOU THE REASON FOR MY BEING HERE

BERESHIT 24:22–33

²²When the camels had finally finished drinking, Avraham's servant took out a gold ring weighting a half-shekel and two bracelets weighing ten shekels. Now he gave these to her as gifts. ²³"Tell me whose daughter you are," he said. "Would your father have room in his house for us to stay overnight?" ²⁴She answered him, "I am the daughter of Bethuel son of Nachor, and Milcah is my mother. ²⁵As for room to stay overnight, that is available, and there is plenty of straw and feed for the camels." ²⁶The man bowed his head in thanksgiving to

---

22. TWO BRACELETS WEIGHING TEN SHEKELS.

וּשְׁנֵי צְמִידִים עַל־יָדֶיהָ עֲשָׂרָה זָהָב מִשְׁקָלָם

The Midrash tells us that the two bracelets represented the two Tablets of the Law, while the weight of ten shekels represented the Ten Commandments, which were inscribed on the two Tablets of the Law.

23. WOULD YOUR FATHER HAVE ROOM IN HIS HOUSE FOR US TO STAY OVERNIGHT?

הַגִּידִי נָא לִי הֲיֵשׁ בֵּית־אָבִיךְ מָקוֹם לָנוּ לָלִין

Eliezer wished to see whether Rivkah's father was as hospitable as she.

25. THERE IS PLENTY OF STRAW AND FEED FOR THE CAMELS.

גַּם־תֶּבֶן גַּם־מִסְפּוֹא רַב עִמָּנוּ

Here again Rivkah shows her concern for the animals by first mentioning the food for them and then a place for Eliezer to sleep.

the Almighty. ²⁷Then he said, "Blessed be the Almighty, God of my master Avraham, Who had been so kind to him. For certainly it has been the Almighty Who has led me straight to my master's family!" ²⁸Meanwhile, the girl ran home to tell her mother what had happened. ²⁹Now, Rivkah had a brother, Lavan. ³⁰When Rivkah came home, Lavan quickly noticed the ring and the bracelets on his sister. He also heard her tell about her conversation with the man. So he rushed off to the well, where he found the man with his camels. ³¹"Come, stay with us," said Lavan. "We certainly have room for you and your camels, you blessed man." ³²So the man came to the house. There the camels were unloaded and were given straw and feed. Then the man and his helpers were given water with which to wash their feet. ³³But when the food was placed before him, the man said, "I will not eat before I tell you the reason for my being here." And they answered him, "Please do so."

---

30. SO HE RUSHED OFF TO THE WELL.

וַיָּרָץ לָבָן אֶל־הָאִישׁ הַחוּצָה אֶל־הָעָיִן

Greedy Lavan was so impressed with the gifts Eliezer gave Rivkah that he ran to greet him.

33. I WILL NOT EAT BEFORE I TELL YOU THE REASON FOR MY BEING HERE.

לֹא אֹכַל עַד אִם־דִּבַּרְתִּי דְּבָרָי

Eliezer put the success of his mission and his loyalty to Avraham above his personal comfort.

Answer " כֵּן " or " לֹא "

1. Avraham's servant gave Rivkah a gold ring. _____

2. The two gold bracelets that Avraham's servant gave to Rivkah weighed five shekels. _____

3. Avraham's servant asked if he could stay at Rivkah's home overnight. _____

4. Rivkah was not related to Avraham. _____

5. Rivkah's mother was named Nachor. _____

Answer the Questions

1. Was Rivkah hospitable in this story, too?

2. Was she kind to animals?

3. Whom did Avraham's servant thank for leading him to his master's family?

4. Who was Rivkah's brother?

5. Did Avraham's servant eat right away when food was placed before him?

Ideas to Explore

1. Why do you think the Torah mentions the weight of the jewelry Avraham's servant gave to Rivkah?

2. Why do you think that Lavan rushed to invite Avraham's servant home? Was his hospitality genuine?

3. Why wouldn't Avraham's servant eat before he told his story?

The People of the Book עַם הַסֵּפֶר

עַם הַסֵּפֶר "People of the book." Have you ever heard the Jewish people called "the people of the book"? This expression is used to mean that we are a studious people with a great love of learning and respect for education. Even though Jews make up only a small part of the population, there are a very large number of scholars, doctors, and scientists among us. In fact, many Nobel Prize winners have been Jews.

But this tradition of scholarship in every area goes back to the original meaning of עַם הַסֵּפֶר. Our סֵפֶר is the Torah , and we Jews are the people of the Torah. In the Torah we find our history, our laws, and our traditions. It is the Torah that binds us together as a people. So we study the Torah every chance we get—reading a Torah portion in the synagogue each Sabbath and each holiday. Torah verses are even contained in the prayers we chant every morning, afternoon, and evening.

And from our study of the greatest book ever written, we learn to love and study other books and to bring their light into our lives, as well.

וַתָּקׇם רִבְקָה וְנַעֲרֹתֶיהָ
וַתִּרְכַּבְנָה עַל־הַגְּמַלִּים וַתֵּלַכְנָה

SO THE SERVANT TOOK RIVKAH AND THEY WERE ON THEIR WAY

[34]"I am Avraham's servant," he began. [35]"The Almighty has blessed my master generously. He has given him sheep and cattle, silver and gold, men and women servants, camels and donkeys. [36]Then in her old age, Sarah, my master's wife, gave birth to their son. And my master has given him everything he owns. [37]But my master made me swear, saying, 'Although we live here in Canaan, you must not let my son marry a Canaanite girl. [38]Instead you are to go to my family and there get a wife for my son.'

[42]"Today, when I arrived at the well, I said, 'Almighty, God of my master Avraham, please bless my mission!' [45]Well, I had hardly finished praying when Rivkah came along with the water jug on her shoulder. So when she went down to draw water from the well, I said to her, 'Please give me a drink.' [46]She quickly lowered her jug

---

45. WELL, I HAD HARDLY FINISHED PRAYING WHEN RIVKAH CAME ALONG.

אֲנִי טֶרֶם אֲכַלֶּה לְדַבֵּר אֶל־לִבִּי וְהִנֵּה רִבְקָה יֹצֵאת

Rivkah was like a beautiful rose growing among thorns. Her father was Bethuel the Aramean and her brother was Lavan, a thief and a cheat. Despite her surroundings, she did not follow in the footsteps of her father and her brother. Her honesty, godliness, and holiness were as great as Yitzchak's.

and said, 'Drink, and I will also give water to your camels.' ⁴⁷Then I asked her, 'Whose daughter are you?' And she said, 'Nachor's daughter. My father is Bethuel son of Nachor, and my mother is Milcah.' So I gave her the ring and the bracelets. ⁴⁸In thanksgiving to the Almighty, I bowed down and blessed the God of my master Avraham, Who led me on the right way to find a girl in his brother's family for my master's son. ⁴⁹Now tell me whether you wish to be kind to my master. If your answer is 'No,' I will decide what to do next."

⁵⁰Lavan and Bethuel answered him, "This must have been decided by the Almighty, and we are willing to accept it without debate. ⁵¹Here is Rivkah. Take her with you and let her become the wife of your master's son, as the Almighty has decided."

⁵²When Avraham's servant heard their answer, he fell to his knees before the Almighty. ⁵³He brought out gifts of silver and gold, and clothing, which he gave to Rivkah. He gave presents also to her mother and brother. And they called Rivkah, and they said to her, "Will you go with this man?" And she said, "Yes, I will go."

⁶¹Then Rivkah and her maid-servants mounted the camels and followed the man. So the servant took Rivkah and they were on their way.

---

50. THIS MUST HAVE BEEN DECIDED BY THE ALMIGHTY.

מֵיהוָה יָצָא הַדָּבָר

Since it was God who brought you and our daughter together, our personal wishes are not important in this matter.

Complete the Sentence

1. The Lord blessed Avraham with sheep and
   _____, silver and _____, men and _____ servants, camels and _____.
2. When she was old, _____ gave birth to a son.
3. Avraham gave everything he owned to _____.

Yitzchak, cattle, women, Sarah, gold, donkeys

Answer the Questions

1. Did Avraham's servant tell Rivkah's family the whole story of his mission?
2. What relation was Rivkah to Yitzchak?
3. How did Avraham's servant put his proposal? What words did he use?
4. What was the answer of Lavan and Bethuel?
5. What did Avraham's servant do when he heard their answer?
6. Was Rivkah from a poor family? How can you tell?
7. Did anyone consult Rivkah about the marriage? When?
8. Who arranged the marriage?

Ideas to Explore

1. Why do you think that Avraham's servant was careful to tell the family about Avraham's and Yitzchak's wealth?
2. From the way that Avraham's servant acts in this story, what kind of a man would you say he was?
3. Why do you think Avraham wanted to find a wife for his son among his own family?
4. What can you tell about "women's lib" in Rivkah's time?

Marriage חֲתֻנָּה

In Bible days marriages were arranged by the parents of the young people. In this Bible story the marriage was arranged by Avraham and Eliezer on one side and Lavan, Milcah, and Bethuel on the other side. Only after the arrangements were completed, was Rivkah consulted.

In the Middle Ages and in Eastern Europe marriages were arranged by a marriage broker called a *shadchan*. The parents felt that the young people were too young and too immature to be entrusted with so serious a decision. The father of the boy or girl would then instruct the *shadchan* to find a mate for his child who would possess desirable qualities' of character and family background.

The *shadchan* would then suggest candidates. After much thought and discussion, the parents would then choose the most desirable mate. Through a *shadchan*, a meeting would be arranged with the prospect's parents and the youngsters. When all were satisfied, the family would conclude the arrangements. The *shadchan* received a percentage of the marriage dowry as a fee for his labor.

Years ago travel and communications between villages were very difficult. Jewish boys and girls had great difficulty meeting suitable partners. The *shadchan* knew many people in different villages, and he was in an ideal position to make recommendations and introductions.

Today, travel and communication are much easier and young people do not need the help of a *shadchan*.

Today, young people do their own selecting. They meet in synagogues, at school, and at work, and choose their own mate.

Selecting a life's partner is a task which one should undertake with great care. Religion, character, a sharing of taste, agreement on goals, family background, and personality are the factors on which one can build a good marriage. These are qualities, which cannot always be judged easily or quickly.

1. Who arranged Rivkah's marriage?
2. Why did Eliezer give Rivkah presents?
3. Why was it necessary to have a *shadchan*?
4. How do young people meet today?
5. How did your parents meet?
6. How long did they date?

RIVKAH SAW YITZCHAK

BERESHIT 24:62–67

[62]In the meanwhile, Yitzchak came up from the Negev where he was living, to Be'er-lahai-roi. [63]One day, during early evening, while he was taking a walk in the countryside, he saw camels coming. [64]Rivkah saw Yitzchak, and she quickly got down from her camel. [65]"Who is that man over there in the field walking toward us?" she asked the servant. "He is my master," the servant answered her. Now she covered her face with a veil.

[66]The servant told Yitzchak everything that had happened. [67]Then Yitzchak brought Rivkah to the tent of his mother, Sarah, and she became his wife. Yitzchak loved her, and she comforted him for the loss of his mother.

---

67. THEN YITZCHAK BROUGHT RIVKAH TO THE TENT OF HIS MOTHER, SARAH.

וַיְבִאֶהָ יִצְחָק הָאֹהֱלָה שָׂרָה אִמּוֹ

Avraham and his beloved wife, Sarah, lived together for many happy years. Our wise Sages tell us that during all those years a cloud of holiness floated over Sarah's tent, night and day. When Sarah died the cloud disappeared.

Then one day, Yitzchak, son of Sarah and Avraham, brought his bride, Rivkah, to his mother's tent. Lo and behold! The cloud reappeared and once more floated over the tent.

Then Yitzchak knew that Rivkah was truly worthy to be his wife and become a part of the family of Avraham.

67. YITZCHAK LOVED HER.   וַיֶּאֱהָבֶהָ יִצְחָק

When Yitzchak and Rivkah looked at each other, they both knew right away that it was God's will that they marry each other. It was love at first sight.

[7]Avraham lived to the age of 175. [8]He died at a good old age, a contented man. [9]His sons, Yitzchak and Yishmael, buried him in the Cave of Machpelah, in the field near Mamre. [10]Avraham was buried next to his wife, Sarah, in the field which he had bought from the Chethites. [11]After Avraham's death, God blessed his son Yitzchak. Yitzchak now lived near Be'er-lahai-roi.

---

67. AND SHE COMFORTED HIM FOR THE LOSS OF HIS MOTHER.

וַיִּנָּחֵם יִצְחָק אַחֲרֵי אִמּוֹ

Yitzchak loved his mother very much. Rivkah filled the loneliness caused by his mother's death. Now once again, their house truly became a home.

9. HIS SONS, YITZCHAK AND YISHMAEL, BURIED HIM IN THE CAVE OF MACHPELAH.

וַיִּקְבְּרוּ אֹתוֹ יִצְחָק וְיִשְׁמָעֵאל בָּנָיו

The brothers forget their rivalry and were united in sorrow as they buried their father. Yishmael repented of his evil ways and behaved toward Yitzchak as a brother should.

Answer " כֵּן " or " לֹא "

1. Yitzchak had been living in Beer-lahai-roi._____
2. Yitzchak came up to the Negev.   _____
3. When Rivkah saw Yitzchak, she quickly got down from her camel.   _____
4. She asked the servant who was approaching.

          _____
5. When she heard it was Yitzchak, she lifted up her veil.   _____

Answer the Questions

1. Did Yitzchak and Rivkah have a wedding ceremony like we have today?
2. Who comforted Yitzchak for the loss of his mother?
3. How old was Avraham when he died?
4. Where was Avraham buried?
5. Who buried him?

Ideas to Explore

1. This is the story of an arranged marriage, but in some ways it is a romantic love story. Do you agree? Why or why not?
2. From this story, how was marriage different in Yitzchak and Rivkah's day?
3. Avraham was buried by both his sons. What does this tell you about Yishmael and his relationship to Yitzchak at this time?

Kaddish קַדִּישׁ

AVRAHAM LIVED TO THE AGE OF 175. HE DIED AT A GOOD OLD AGE. . . HIS SONS, YITZCHAK AND YISHMAEL, BURIED HIM.

In Talmudic times those carrying the coffin from the road to the grave site would pause seven times. The Rabbis explain that the seven stops correspond to the seven days of Creation. After the coffin has been placed in the grave, a short burial service (צְדּוּק הַדִּין) is recited. In it we acknowledge God's wisdom, accept the final judgment, and affirm our belief in the eternity of the soul. The closing words are from the Book of Job:

"The Almighty gave, the Almighty has taken away.
Blessed be the name of the Almighty."

יְיָ נָתַן וַיְיָ לָקָח

יְהִי שֵׁם יְיָ מְבֹרָךְ:

Job 1:21

As the צְדּוּק הַדִּין concludes, the mourners recite the קַדִּישׁ for the first time. A Jew remembers loved ones who have passed on by reciting this ancient hymn of praise. In praising God, the mourner accepts the plan of God's universe, acknowledging that death is an inevitable part of human life. In years gone by קַדִּישׁ was recited only by children for their parents; however, today קַדִּישׁ is said also for a child, brother, sister, husband, or wife.

The grave is then covered. The task is begun by members of the family, then completed by friends. As the family of the deceased leaves the cemetery, those assembled express their sympathy and consolation in the traditional formula:

"May you be comforted among the mourners for Zion and Jerusalem."

הַמָּקוֹם יְנַחֶמְךָ (יְנַחֵם אֶתְכֶם)

בְּתוֹךְ שְׁאָר אֲבֵלֵי צִיּוֹן וִירוּשָׁלָיִם:

וְהִנֵּה תוֹמִם בְּבִטְנָהּ

SHE GAVE BIRTH TO TWINS

[19]This is the story of Yitzchak son of Avraham. [20]Yitzchak was 40 years old when he married Rivkah, the daughter of Bethuel the Aramean from Paddan-aram, sister of Lavan. [21]Yitzchak prayed to the Almighty to give Rivkah a child, and the Almighty answered his prayer. Rivkah became pregnant. [22]But it seemed as if children were punching each other inside her. "If this continues," she cried, "I shall not be able to take it!" And she prayed to the Almighty. [23]The Almighty answered her.

[24]When the time for delivery came, she gave birth to twins. [25]The first was born with reddish hair over him. It was as if he were wearing a fox-skin. They called him "Esav." [26]Next was born the other twin, with his hand

---

22. IT SEEMED AS IF CHILDREN WERE PUNCHING EACH OTHER.

וַיִּתְרֹצְצוּ הַבָּנִים בְּקִרְבָּהּ

The two punching children, Esav and Yaakov, would become two nations, Edom and Yisrael. The two children would not be on friendly terms with each other, and neither would the two nations. And so it was, Israel and Edom were constantly at war with each other.

Esav was just a few minutes older than his brother Yaakov. Although the two brothers were twins, they were not alike. Esav was very hairy, and his arms and body were covered with thick red hair. Yaakov's hands and neck were very smooth. Esav grew up to be a strong man, and he loved to hunt in the woods and mountains for deer. But Yaakov was quiet and thoughtful, staying at home and caring for the flocks of his father.

holding on to Esav's heel. They called him, "Yaakov." [27]As the boys grew older, Esav became a very skilled hunter, an outdoorsman. But Yaakov was a quiet type who kept close to home. [28]Yitzchak considered Esav his favorite and enjoyed the venison which Esav brought him. Rivkah favored Yaakov.

[29]One day, when Yaakov was cooking some food, Esav rushed in from the outdoors, hungry and tired. [30]"Give me a helping of that red stuff," he shouted to Yaakov. "I'm starved!" [31]And Yaakov said, "Swap me your birthright for it." [32]"Here I am, dying of hunger!" Esav answered him. "So what good is the birthright to me?" [33]To which Yaakov said, "Give me your solemn promise right now." So Esav swore that he was giving up his birthright to Yaakov. [34]Then Yaakov gave Esav some bread and red-bean stew. He ate, drank, got up and rushed off. In this way did Esav mistreat his birthright.

---

24. SHE GAVE BIRTH TO TWINS. וְהִנֵּה תוֹמִם בְּבִטְנָהּ

Our wise Sages tell us that Yaakov and Esav went to school together until they were thirteen years old. Then Esav left school and became a hunter and a worshipper of idols, but Yaakov continued his studies and was faithful to the God of his father.

As time passed, both brothers became hunters of people. Esav tried to find people who would worship idols, but Yaakov looked for people who would worship the one true God, the God of Israel.

25. THEY CALLED HIM "ESAV." וַיִּקְרְאוּ שְׁמוֹ עֵשָׂו

The name Esav comes from the Hebrew verb עָשָׂה, "to make." Esav was born with as much hair as a "full-made" (mature) man.

Esav had reddish hair over him. Esav's reddish hair was a sign that he and his descendants would shed a great deal of blood.

Match the Columns

1. Yitzchak was forty when he married	Lavan
2. Rivkah was the sister of	the Almighty
3. Rivkah became	punching
4. The children inside her were	pregnant
5. Rivkah prayed to	Rivkah

Answer the Questions

1. What was the red-haired child named?
2. What was unusual about Yaakov's birth?
3. Which son was a hunter and which son was quiet?
4. How did Esav happen to sell his birthright?
5. What food did he sell it for?
6. What is meant by birthright?
7. What are the privileges of the birthright?

Ideas to Explore

1. The Torah tells us that Esav mistreated his birthright. How did he do so?
2. What about Yaakov's part in this story? Do you think that he dealt fairly with Esav?
3. How were the brothers physically different?
4. How were the characters of the brothers different?

What's In A Name?

In ancient times names were given in connection with events in the family, the community, or the world.

Esav comes from the Hebrew word עָשָׂה "to make." Esav was born with as much hair as a "fully-made" mature man.

Yaakov was given his name because he held on to the עָקֵב (heel) of Esav.

Today, among Ashkenazi Jews, it is customary to name the child after a dead relative. Among Sephardim, a child may be named after a living relative.

There is no law regarding the naming of children or how a child's name should be chosen. Custom and sentiment are the determining factors.

1. Do you know how your Hebrew name was chosen?_____
   _____

   יְהוּדָה

   עִירָה

2. Were you named for a relative your parents admired?_____
   _____

   גֵּרְשׁוֹן

   רִינָה

3. Ask your family to recall the ideas or feelings involved in choosing your Hebrew name._____
   _____

   רְאוּבֵן

4. Have you had any nicknames?_____

   אֶפְרַיִם

5. How did you get those names?_____

6. What do these nicknames say about you?_____
   _____

   דָּן
   לֵיאָה

Finding unusual names for a group or a club has become a popular indoor sport. Pretend that your temple is forming a new youth club and they are looking for a name, in Hebrew or in English, to express its identity. Choose a name for your club.

LET ANY CURSE AGAINST YOU BE ON ME, MY SON.

עָלַי קִלְלָתְךָ בְּנִי

¹When Yitzchak was old and nearly blind, he called his older son, Esav, and said to him, "My son!" Esav replied, "Here I am." ²"As you can see, I am an old man," Yitzchak said. "There is no telling when I may die. ³Take your bow and arrows and go out into the fields and get me some venison. ⁴Then prepare it the way I like it and bring it to me to eat, so that I may give you my blessing before I die."

⁵Rivkah had been listening while Yitzchak was talking to Esav. So when Esav left for the field to hunt venison for his father, ⁶Rivkah said to her son Yaakov, "I just overheard your father telling your brother Esav, ⁷'Bring me some venison and prepare it for me that I may eat it and bless you with the Lord's approval before I die.' ⁸Now, my son, do exactly as I command you. ⁹Go out to the flock and bring me two young goats, and I will prepare your father's favorite dish. ¹⁰Then take it to your father to eat,

---

4. SO THAT I MAY GIVE YOU MY BLESSING BEFORE I DIE.

בַּעֲבוּר תְּבָרֶכְךָ נַפְשִׁי בְּטֶרֶם אָמוּת

The instructions given by a dying person have legal and moral worth and were to be carried out by the survivors. Today people write wills in which they give instructions about what to do with their money and their property after their death.

The Hebrew word for "will" is צַוָּאָה. The root word is צָוָה, which means "to command." In a צַוָּאָה we command our family to dispose of our earthly goods in a special way.

so that he may bless you before he dies." [11]"But my brother Esav," said Yaakov to his mother, "is a hairy man, while my skin is very smooth! [12]If my father touches me, I will look to him like a trickster, and I will bring on me a curse instead of a blessing." [13]His mother answered him, "Let any curse against you be on me, my son! Just do what I tell you. Go, get me the goats."
[14]So he went, got them, and brought them to his mother. She prepared his father's favorite dish. [15]Then Rivkah took the best clothes of her older son, Esav, and put them on her younger son, Yaakov. [16]She next covered up his hands and the hairless part of his neck with the hairy skin of young goats. [17]She then gave her son Yaakov the tasty dish and the bread that she had prepared.

---

8. DO EXACTLY AS I COMMAND YOU.

שְׁמַע בְּקֹלִי לַאֲשֶׁר אֲנִי מְצַוָּה אֹתָךְ

The noun is מִצְוָה, "commandment." Every Jewish boy and girl becomes a בַּר מִצְוָה or בַּת מִצְוָה at the age of thirteen This means "one who is obliged to obey the commandments."

Why should the word מִצְוָה, "commandment," also mean "good deed"? Quite obviously the commandments written down in the Bible are all good deeds.

13. LET ANY CURSE AGAINST YOU BE ON ME.

עָלַי קִלְלָתְךָ בְּנִי

A devoted mother will often place her child's happiness before her own.

17. SHE THEN GAVE HER SON YAAKOV THE TASTY DISH AND THE BREAD THAT SHE HAD PREPARED.

וַתִּתֵּן אֶת־הַמַּטְעַמִּים וְאֶת־הַלֶּחֶם אֲשֶׁר עָשָׂתָה

Rivkah, with a mother's feeling for her children, knew that Esav was not fit to receive the blessing and become the father of a great nation. She knew that Yaakov was a serious God-fearing man who would carry on with the family tradition.

Answer "כֵּן" or "לֹא"

1. When Yitzchak was old he saw very well. _____
2. Yitzchak asked Esav to prepare him some venison. _____
3. Rivkah told Esav to pretend to be Yaakov. _____
4. Rivkah gave Yaakov Esav's clothes to wear and goat skin to cover up his hands. _____

Ideas to Explore

1. Why do you suppose that Rivkah decided to fool Yitzchak and get Esav's blessing for Yaakov?
2. Because Yitzchak was old and nearly blind, do you think that Rivkah knew her sons better than Yitzchak did?
3. Who prepared food in this family—men, women, or both?

What Do You Think?

1. Yitzchak prepares for death by blessing his sons. Would you prepare for death if you were very old? How?
2. If you were a parent and you loved one child more than another, how would you act towards your children?

The Nobel Prizes פְּרָסֵי-נוֹבֶּל

Esav was a hunter who was happy killing animals and destroying life. Yaakov was just the opposite. He was a peaceful man who kept close to home and was interested in making life happier for humanity.

There are many people such as Esav, who love to destroy and kill. Fortunately, there are also untold numbers of quiet people with special ideas, such as Yaakov.

The Yaakovs invent new machinery, discover medicines, paint beautiful pictures, write interesting books study Torah, and compose wonderful music. Yaakovs do many things to make our lives holier, happier, healthier and more interesting.

Alfred Nobel (1883–1896) was a Swedish ammunition manufacturer who believed in the future of humanity. When he died, he left millions of dollars to establish five annual prizes: for outstanding achievement in the fields of peace, physics, chemistry, medicine, and literature. Each prize consists of a gold medal and a cash award from the Nobel Foundation. Since the start of the prizes in 1899, they have been awarded to more than 400 Yaakovs. Of these, more than one-third have been Jews.

ARE YOU REALLY MY SON, ESAV? אַתָּה זֶה בְּנִי עֵשָׂו

BERESHIT 27:18–29

¹⁸He now came to his father and said, "Father!" "Yes?" he said. "But which one of my sons are you?" ¹⁹And Yaakov said to his father, "I am Esav, your first-born. I have done as you told me. Please, sit up and eat of my venison, that you may give me your very own blessing." ²⁰Yitzchak asked, "But how were you able to find it so quickly, my son?" He answered, "Because the Almighty your God was helpful to me." ²¹Then Yitzchak said to Yaakov, "Come closer so that I can touch you, my son, and be sure whether you are my son Esav or not."

---

18. BUT WHICH ONE OF MY SONS ARE YOU? מִי אַתָּה בְּנִי

Yitzchak was suspicious of the speed with which "Esav" had prepared the meal and by his respectful replies. Besides, the voice sounded like that of Yaakov. Blind people have a highly developed sense of hearing.

20. BUT HOW WERE YOU ABLE TO FIND IT SO QUICKLY?

מַה־זֶּה מִהַרְתָּ לִמְצֹא

Esav had to go hunting, kill an animal, bring it home, and cook it. Yaakov took the animal from his herd and prepared the meal very quickly.

20. BECAUSE THE ALMIGHTY . . . WAS HELPFUL TO ME.

כִּי הִקְרָה יְהוָה אֱלֹהֶיךָ לְפָנָי

The Rabbis tell us that Yaakov was very surprised to hear the name of God from the lips of the man who called himself Esav. He knew from bitter experience that Esav was not religious and rarely spoke of God.

²²Yaakov came up closer to his father, Yitzchak, who felt him and said, "The voice is the voice of Yaakov, but the hands are the hands of Esav." ²³He did not recognize him because his hands were hairy, like those of his brother Esav. He was ready to bless him. ²⁴But, suddenly, he asked again, "Are you really my son Esav?" "I am," he answered. ²⁵So Yitzchak now said, "Serve it to me, my son, that I may eat of the venison and give you my very own blessing." He served it to him, and he ate. He brought him some wine, and he drank.

²⁶Then his father Yitzchak said to him, "Come closer, my son, and kiss me." ²⁷He came close and Yitzchak kissed him. As he smelled the odor of his clothes, he blessed him, saying:

> "Ah, the fragrance of my son
> Is like the fragrance of a field
> Which the Almighty has blessed.

²⁸May God give you
> Of the dew of heaven
> And the richness of the earth
> Plenty of new grain and wine.

²⁹Let nations serve you,
> Peoples bow before you.
> Be master of your brother;
> Let your mother's sons bow before you."

---

22. THE VOICE IS THE VOICE OF YAAKOV, BUT THE HANDS ARE THE HANDS OF ESAV.

הַקֹּל קוֹל יַעֲקֹב וְהַיָּדַיִם יְדֵי עֵשָׂו

Much of the history of the Jewish people has been the struggle between the hands of Esav, power and strength, and the voice of Yaakov, study, peace, and devotion to Torah.

The Rabbis say that so long as the voice of the Jews can be heard studying and praying, the Children of Israel will never be defeated by the hands of Esav.

Match the Columns

1. Esav's father was   Yaakov

2. Yitzchak was married to   Esav

3. Yitzchak's firstborn was   Rivkah

4. Rivkah's favorite son was   Yitzchak

Answer the Questions

1. Was Yitzchak immediately suspicious that this was not Esav? How can you tell?
2. Did Yaakov take as long to bring the venison as a hunter would have?
3. What senses did Yitzchak use to try to figure out which son was serving him?
4. Did Yitzchak bless Yaakov?
5. What did Yitzchak wish for Yaakov in the blessing?

Ideas to Explore

1. Did Yaakov do the right thing in taking Esav's blessing? Why or why not? Remember that Esav had sold Yaakov his birthright.
2. Who do you think undertood the children better—Yitzchak or Rivkah? Why?
3. It was after Yaakov talked about God's help that Yitzchak said his voice was not Esav's. Do you think that Yitzchak was influenced by what Yaakov said, and not just his voice?

The Five Senses

God gave us five senses with which to appreciate the wonders and beauty of the world: hearing, seeing, touching, smelling, and tasting. All day long we use these marvelous gifts of God.

We taste the delicious foods of the world with our ⎯⎯⎯⎯⎯

We smell the odors of the world with our ⎯⎯⎯⎯⎯

We see the beauty of the world with our ⎯⎯⎯⎯⎯

We hear the wonders of the world with our ⎯⎯⎯⎯⎯

We touch the marvels of the world with our ⎯⎯⎯⎯⎯

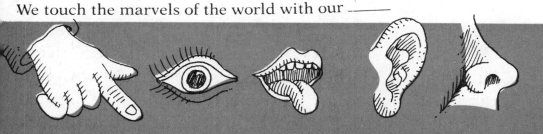

Here are several quotations from the Bible story. Name the senses used in these activities. Which parts of the body were used? Write your answers in Hebrew or in English.

"Come closer so that I can touch you."
"The voice is the voice of Yaakov."
"The hands are the hands of Esav."
"Please sit up and eat of my venison."
"The fragrance of my son."

THINK OF SOME THINGS YOU HEARD, SMELLED, TOUCHED, OR SAW TODAY.

⎯⎯⎯⎯⎯⎯⎯⎯⎯⎯⎯⎯⎯⎯⎯⎯⎯⎯⎯⎯⎯⎯⎯⎯⎯⎯⎯⎯⎯

⎯⎯⎯⎯⎯⎯⎯⎯⎯⎯⎯⎯⎯⎯⎯   ⎯⎯⎯⎯⎯

וַיִּשְׂטֹם עֵשָׂו אֶת־יַעֲקֹב

SO ESAV HATED YAAKOV

[30]No sooner had Yaakov left his father, Yitzchak, after the blessing, than his brother Esav came back from hunting. [31]He also prepared his father's favorite dish and brought it to him. "Sit up, father," he said, "and eat of your son's venison, so that you may give me your very own blessing." [32]"Who are you?" his father asked. "I am Esav, your oldest son!" he answered. [33]Yitzchak was terribly disturbed, and he asked, "Then who was it that hunted the venison and has already brought it to me? I finished eating it just before you came and I blessèd him. And now it is he who must remain blessed." [34]Having heard his father's words, Esav broke out with wild and bitter sobbing. "Bless me, too, father," he pleaded. [35]But he answered, "Your brother came here with trickery and carried off your blessing." [36]"No wonder they called him 'Yaakov'!" Esav cried out, "Twice he tricked me! First he took away my birthright, and now he has taken away my blessing. Have you saved no blessing for me?" [37]But Yitzchak answered Esav, "I have already made him master over you. I have given him all his tribesmen as servants. I have assured him plenty of grain and wine. What can I now give to you, my son?" [38]"Have you only one blessing?" Esav

---

36. HE TOOK AWAY MY BIRTHRIGHT.   אֶת־בְּכֹרָתִי לָקָח

Esav, conveniently forgetting that he had sold the birthright fair and square, accuses Yaakov of stealing the birthright.

asked his father. "Bless me also!" Esav pleaded tearfully. ³⁹Then Yitzchak said to him:

"Away from the richness of the earth
And from the dew above shall your home be.
⁴⁰By your sword shall you live,
And you shall serve your brother.
But when you become restless,
You shall throw off his yoke and be free."

⁴¹So Esav hated Yaakov because of the blessing his father had given to him. Esav said to himself, "When my father is gone and the time of mourning has come, I will kill my brother Yaakov." ⁴²When these words of her older son Esav were reported to Rivkah, she called her younger son Yaakov and said to him, "Your brother Esav is planning revenge against you. ⁴³Listen to me now, my son. Flee immediately to my brother, Lavan, in Haran. ⁴⁴Stay with him a while, until your brother's anger is gone.

---

40. BY YOUR SWORD SHALL YOU LIVE. וְעַל־חַרְבְּךָ תִחְיֶה

Esav and his descendants lived in the barren land of Edom. They earned their living as nomadic hunters and shepherds.

41. ESAV SAID TO HIMSELF, "WHEN MY FATHER IS GONE AND THE TIME OF MOURNING HAS COME."

יִקְרְבוּ יְמֵי אֵבֶל אָבִי

Esav was anxious to kill Yaakov, but to his credit he did not wish to cause his dying father any more grief. He decided to postpone his revenge until after his father's death.

44. STAY WITH HIM A WHILE, UNTIL YOUR BROTHER'S ANGER IS GONE.

וְיָשַׁבְתָּ עִמּוֹ יָמִים אֲחָדִים עַד אֲשֶׁר־תָּשׁוּב חֲמַת אָחִיךָ

Rivkah tried to act as a peacemaker. She hoped that in time Esav's anger would disappear and the two brothers would become friends once again.

114

Answer " כֵּן " or " לֹא "

1. Esav prepared the dish his father didn't like. _____
2. Yitzchak figured out that he had given Esav's blessing to Yaakov. _____
3. Esav didn't mind a bit. _____
4. Yitzchak did not bless Esav. _____
5. Esav threatened to kill Yaakov. _____
6. Rivkah sent Yaakov to stay with her father. _____

Ideas to Explore

1. Did Esav love his father? Give evidence to support your answer.
2. Once blessed, Yaakov had to remain blessed, even if he received the blessing "with trickery." Do you think this was fair? Why do you think Yitzchak felt this way?

What Do You Think?

1. It seems that Esav was Yitzchak's favorite, while Yaakov was Rivkah's favorite. Do you think that parents sometimes do love one of their children more than another? What problems can this cause?
2. Do you think that mothers should be willing to sacrifice themselves for their children? If you were a mother, would you be?
3. As a mark of respect, Yaakov dressed in the best clothes before going to see his father. How do you show respect for your parents?

Feelings

Esav was angry at Yaakov and wanted to kill him. Rivkah hoped that in a few days Esav's anger would disappear and the brothers would once again become friends.

It is normal and natural to all people of all ages to feel anger, sadness, shyness, fright, bravery, and cowardice. It is normal and natural to be curious, to wonder, to feel bored, to lose your temper and to feel guilty afterwards.

At the same time, people are also different. While we all have these feelings, some have more of one kind than the other. Some people's feelings make them behave one way while the same feelings will make somebody else behave in an altogether different way.

No two people really look exactly alike. Even twins, who may seem to be the same, will each have something that is different about them. The same is true of feelings. Each person's feelings are special in some way.

Feelings influence just about everything we do. They affect the way we think about ourselves and about other people. They affect the way we behave. Understanding our feelings can help us to decide what we want to do about them.

Define these feeling words in terms of what they mean to you.

Happiness is	Bravery is
Anger is	Sadness is

וְהָיָה זַרְעֲךָ כַּעֲפַר הָאָרֶץ

YOUR DESCENDANTS SHALL BE LIKE THE DUST OF THE EARTH

BERESHIT 28:1–22 ¹So Yitzchak called Yaakov and blessed him. He instructed him, saying, "You shall not marry a Canaanite woman. ²Instead, go to Paddan-aram, to the house of your mother's father, Bethuel, and marry one of your Uncle Lavan's daughters. ³And may God Almighty bless you with many children. May you grow into a great nation of many people. ⁴May God pass on to you and to your descendants the blessing of Avraham. So that you come to own this land in which we are immigrants, but which God had promised to Avraham." ⁵Then Yitzchak sent Yaakov away. He went to Paddan-aram, to his Uncle Lavan, Rivkah's brother and the son of Bethuel the Aramean.

---

1. SO YITZCHAK CALLED YAAKOV AND BLESSED HIM.

וַיִּקְרָא יִצְחָק אֶל־יַעֲקֹב וַיְבָרֶךְ אֹתוֹ

Yitzchak realizes that he has blessed Yaakov. Inwardly, he knows that he has blessed the right son and that the future of the Hebrew people is in good hands. Now Yitzchak once again, and this time knowingly, blesses Yaakov.

3. MAY YOU GROW INTO A GREAT NATION OF MANY PEOPLE.

וַיַּפְרְךָ וְיַרְבֶּךָ וְהָיִיתָ לִקְהַל עַמִּים

God had promised that the children of Avraham would become a great nation. Now Yitzchak gives Yaakov the same blessing.

Years later the twelve tribes of Israel would call Yaakov (renamed Yisrael) their father.

¹⁰Meanwhile, Yaakov left Be'er-sheba and headed for Haran. ¹¹He arrived at a certain place at sundown and stayed there for the night. He took one of the rocks of the place, put it under his head, and went to sleep. ¹²He had a dream in which a stairway reached from the ground to the sky and angels of God were going up and down on it. ¹³The Almighty was standing above him. The Almighty said, "I am the Almighty, the God of your forefather Avraham and the God of Yitzchak. The ground on which you are lying, I will give to you and to your descendants. ¹⁵Remember, I am with you; I will protect you wherever you go. I will bring you back to this land."

¹⁸Early next morning, Yaakov took the rock which had been under his head and set it up as a memorial pillar. Over it he poured oil. ¹⁹He called the place Beth-El. The former name of that town had been Luz.

²⁰Yaakov then made a vow, saying, "If God is with me and protects me on this journey, and gives me food and clothes, ²¹and a safe return to my father's house, the Almighty shall be my God. ²²And this stone which I have set up as a memorial pillar shall be a House of God. Here will I offer to You one-tenth of all with which You bless me.

22. HERE WILL I OFFER TO YOU ONE–TENTH OF ALL WITH WHICH YOU BLESS ME.

וְכֹל אֲשֶׁר תִּתֶּן־לִי עַשֵּׂר אֲעַשְּׂרֶנּוּ לָךְ

Yaakov is grateful to God and promises to give one-tenth (tithe) of his earnings to the poor every year. In ancient Israel, the Jews were required to give מַעֲשֵׂר (one-tenth of their crops) to charity. There are many laws in the Talmud dealing with (מַעֲשֵׂר) Today, there are many Jews all over the world who contribute a tithe מַעֲשֵׂר of their earnings to charity. When you give a "tithe, you are thanking God for watching over us and giving us a share of the world's wealth.

Complete the Sentence

1. Yitzchak told Yaakov to marry one of the daughters of _____.
2. Yitzchak blessed Yaakov with the blessing of _____.
3. Yaakov set out for _____.
4. Yaakov had a strange _____.
5. He dreamed of a stairway that reached from the ground to the _____.

dream, Paddan-aram, Avraham, sky, Lavan

Answer the Questions

1. Who went up and down the stairway in Yaakov's dream?
2. What did God promise Yaakov in his dream?
3. What did Yaakov do with the rock that served as his pillow?
4. What did Yaakov name the place?
5. What did Yaakov promise God?

Ideas to Explore

1. Yitzchak had already given Esav's blessing to Yaakov. Now he blesses him again. Do you think that Yitzchak always intended to give Yaakov this blessing?
2. How is Yaakov's blessing different from the blessing Yitzchak had intended for Esav?
3. Both Avraham and Yitzchak told their sons not to marry a Canaanite woman. What does this tell you about the Canaanite women and about Judaism?
4. What do you think Yaakov's dream meant?

Whom Will You Support?

Suppose that when you become an adult, you decide to "tithe" your earnings. How would you distribute your money?

Look at this community map. Decide which three places will receive your support. Tell why you would contribute to those institutions.

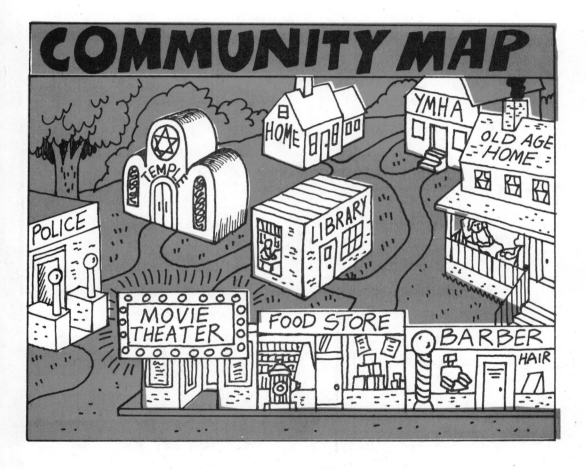

I would support the_____because_____
_____.

I would support the_____because_____
_____.

I would support the_____because_____
_____.

עַצְמִי וּבְשָׂרִי אָתָּה

YOU ARE MY FLESH AND BLOOD

BERESHIT
29:1–12

¹Yaakov traveled on, until he arrived in the land of the Kedemites. ²As he looked around, he saw three flocks of sheep lying near a well, waiting to be watered. But a large stone covered the mouth of the well. ³When all the flocks were there, the stone would be removed from the mouth of the well. Then the stone would be put back into place.

⁴Yaakov said to them "Brothers, where are you from?" They answered, "We are from Haran." ⁵Then he inquired, "Do you know Lavan, son of Nachor?" And they said, "We do." ⁶He asked further, "Is he well?" They replied, "He is. By chance, his daughter is now coming with his flock." ⁷"And why don't you water your flocks so that they can get back to pasture?" he asked.

"After all, it is still broad daylight and hardly time yet to round up the sheep." ⁸They answered, "We can't, until all the shepherds get together to remove the stone off the mouth of the well, so that we can water the sheep."

---

4. BROTHERS, WHERE ARE YOU FROM? אַחַי מֵאַיִן אַתֶּם

Yaakov was a stranger in Haran, yet he called the shepherds "brothers." To Yaakov all people, regardless of race, color, or creed, were his brothers.

⁹While he was still talking to them, Rachel arrived with her father's flock, for she was a shepherdess. ¹⁰As soon as Yaakov saw Rachel, the daughter of his Uncle Lavan, with the sheep, he went over and rolled the stone from the mouth of the well. He watered his uncle's flock. ¹¹Then Yaakov kissed Rachel and burst into tears. ¹²Yaakov told Rachel how he was related to her. She quickly ran to tell her father. ¹³When Lavan heard the news about Yaakov, his nephew, he rushed out to greet him.

---

10. HE WENT OVER AND ROLLED THE STONE FROM THE MOUTH OF THE WELL.

וַיָּגֶל אֶת־הָאֶבֶן מֵעַל פִּי הַבְּאֵר

The Torah tells us that when Yaakov arrived in the land of the Kedemites he found many shepherds and their flocks standing around the well. The well was covered by a huge stone. When Yaakov asked the shepherds why they did not water their flocks, the shepherds replied, "The stone which covers our well is so heavy that we need many people to move it." Yaakov walked up to the stone and removed it very easily.

13. HE RUSHED OUT TO GREET HIM.

וַיָּרָץ לִקְרָאתוֹ, וַיְחַבֶּק לוֹ

Lavan remembered Avraham's servant Eliezer, who came with many gifts. Naturally, he expected the same from Yaakov. So Lavan embraced Yaakov to feel whether he had anything hidden on his body. He also kissed Yaakov to find out whether he had any jewels hidden in his mouth.

Complete the Sentences

1. Yaakov traveled on, until he arrived at the land of the _____ .
2. Lavan, son of _____ .
3. Yaakov told _____ how he was related to her.
4. "Do you know _____ son of Nahor?"
5. Rachel was a _____ .

Kedemites, Shepherdess, Nahor, Lavan, Rachel

Answer the Questions

1. Why didn't the shepherds themselves, move the stone which covered the mouth of the well?
2. From what city were the shepherds?
3. Who finally moved the stone from the mouth of the well?
4. Who watered Lavan's sheep?
5. Who rushed up to Yaakov to greet him?

Ideas to Explore

1. Why did Yaakov call the shepherds "brothers?"
2. What makes you think that Yaakov was extremely strong?
3. Why was it necessary to cover the well with a very heavy stone?
4. Lavan had many slaves, yet Rachel worked as a shepherdess. What does that tell you about Rachel's character?
5. Why did Lavan rush to greet Yaakov?

וְאָהַבְתָּ לְרֵעֲךָ כָּמוֹךָ
Love Thy Neighbor

Yaakov was a stranger in Haran, yet he called the shepherds "brothers." To Yaakov all people, regardless of race, color, or creed, were "brothers"—friends and neighbors.

The word "neighbor" does not mean just someone who lives next-door or across the street. It also means someone who sits beside us at school. That person might be very different from you. He might be a he—or she might be a she! He or she may even have different-color skin than yours.

The word "neighbor" also means people who live in other parts of the world. Today, when giant jets can fly people thousands of miles in a very short time, the world has become smaller. When you walk down the street of a modern city, you may see all kinds of people—Indians, Japanese, etc.

It is very easy to be friendly with people who speak the same language we speak, eat the same kind of foods, and play the same kind of games we play—and even go to temple with us. It takes a lot more trying to be friendly to people who do all those things differently from the way we do them.

The mitzvah of friendliness (רֵעוּת) also means visiting the sick, giving charity, and being friendly with old people and really caring about them.

When we meet people from other countries we should be kind and friendly to them, even though they may not speak our language. When we visit other countries, we want people to be friendly to us.

When we obey the Torah law "Love thy neighbor," וְאָהַבְתָּ לְרֵעֲךָ כָּמוֹךָ we are doing our part in making the world a better place in which to live. We are doing our part in bringing peace to all humankind.

וַיֶּאֱהַב יַעֲקֹב אֶת־רָחֵל
YAAKOV LOVED RACHEL

**BERESHIT
29:15–28**

¹⁵After Yaakov had been there about a month, Lavan said to him one day, "Just because you are my relative is no reason why you should work for me without pay. Tell me what your wages shall be." ¹⁶Now Lavan had two daughters. The older was Leah; and the younger, Rachel. ¹⁷Leah had lovely eyes, but Rachel was shapely and beautiful. ¹⁸Yaakov loved Rachel. He answered, therefore, "I will work for you for seven years if you will give me your younger daughter, Rachel, for a wife." ¹⁹Lavan said, "I would much rather give her to you than to any outsider. Stay on with me." ²⁰So Yaakov worked seven years for Rachel. But the years seemed to him like a few

18. I WILL WORK FOR YOU . . . IF YOU WILL GIVE ME YOUR YOUNGER DAUGHTER, RACHEL, FOR A WIFE.

אֶעֱבָדְךָ שֶׁבַע שָׁנִים בְּרָחֵל בִּתְּךָ הַקְּטַנָּה

In those days, and in some places even today, a man must pay the bride's family for the privilege of marrying the daughter. If he cannot pay in money, cattle, or goods, he can offer his labor as a substitute.

20. SO YAAKOV WORKED SEVEN YEARS FOR RACHEL.

וַיַּעֲבֹד יַעֲקֹב בְּרָחֵל שֶׁבַע שָׁנִים

Yaakov agreed to work seven years for Rachel. He did his work honestly and faithfully, and he expected Lavan to be equally honest and faithful in keeping his side of the agreement.

20. BUT THE YEARS SEEMED TO HIM LIKE A FEW DAYS.

וַיִּהְיוּ בְעֵינָיו כְּיָמִים אֲחָדִים

Yaakov was so much in love with Rachel that the seven years flew by very swiftly.

days because he was so much in love with her. [21]Finally, Yaakov said to Lavan, "I have carried out my contract with you. Now give me my wife." [22]So Lavan gathered all of the local people and he made a party. [23]That night, he brought Leah, his daughter, to Yaakov. [25]In the morning, to Yaakov's surprise, he realized that Leah was his bride. Then he said to Lavan, "What have you done to me? Have I not worked for Rachel? Why have you tricked me?" [26]Lavan answered, "It is not the custom in our country to marry off the younger daughter ahead of the elder. [27]Wait until this week of celebration is over and I will also give you my other daughter, in return for another seven years of work."
[28]Yaakov agreed. He waited until the celebration week ended. Then Lavan gave him also his daughter Rachel. He stayed on to work another seven years.

23. THAT NIGHT, HE BROUGHT LEAH, HIS DAUGHTER, TO YAAKOV.

וַיִּקַּח אֶת־לֵאָה בִתּוֹ וַיָּבֵא אֹתָהּ אֵלָיו

Leah was the eldest daughter, and in ancient times it was customary for the eldest daughter to marry first. Lavan veils Leah to make sure that her true identity will be hidden. The wedding ceremony is carried out in the evening, in semi-darkness, and Leah becomes Yaakov's bride. Lavan has fooled Yaakov in the same way that Yaakov fooled his father, Yitzchak. The fooler becomes the fooled.

27. WAIT UNTIL THIS WEEK OF CELEBRATION IS OVER AND I WILL ALSO GIVE YOU MY OTHER DAUGHTER, IN RETURN FOR ANOTHER SEVEN YEARS OF WORK.

מַלֵּא שְׁבֻעַ זֹאת וְנִתְּנָה לְךָ גַּם־אֶת־זֹאת בַּעֲבֹדָה אֲשֶׁר תַּעֲבֹד

After seven days of feasting and celebration in honor of his marriage to Leah, another ceremony is held. This time Yaakov marries Rachel. He is now obligated to work another seven years for Lavan to pay his debt for Rachel.

Marrying several wives is called polygamy. In ancient days it was permitted to have several wives.

Complete the Sentence

1. At first, Yaakov worked for one month without _____.
2. Then _____ offered to pay Yaakov.
3. Lavan's older daughter was _____.
4. Lavan's younger daughter was _____.
5. Leah had lovely _____.

Lavan, Rachel, Leah, pay, eyes

Answer the Questions

1. Who was prettier, Leah or Rachel?
2. For which daughter did Yaakov offer to work seven years?
3. Did Lavan agree?
4. How did Lavan trick Yaakov?
5. What was Lavan's explanation for his trick?
6. In all, how many years did Yaakov work for Rachel?

Ideas to Explore

1. Do you think that Lavan took advantage of Yaakov by having him work without pay?
2. Should Lavan have accepted Yaakov's offer to work for seven years for Rachel? Why or why not?
3. How do we know that Yaakov loved Rachel?
4. Just as Lavan tricked Yaakov, Yaakov had tricked Yitzchak. Do you see some justice in Yaakov's being tricked?
5. When Yaakov was given Leah for a bride, he carried on with the wedding celebrations and agreed to work another seven years for Rachel. What kind of man was he?

Modesty and Conceit

Yaakov did his work honestly and faithfully. The Midrash tells us that Lavan's flocks increased five times as much while Yaakov was the shepherd.

Yaakov did not brag about his accomplishments. He was an עָנָו —a modest person. He did not brag about his accomplishments. Yaakov just did his work and did it well.

People who brag are really a drag!

Nobody likes a conceited person who is always bragging about all the great things he or she can do. We all know people who keep talking about how smart they are or how much money they have. Their favorite word is "tomorrow." They say they are going to do great things—not today but tomorrow. Then when tomorrow comes, they say they will do great things next week or next year. This kind of a person is called a בַּעַל גַּאֲוָה (a conceited person).

A person who really does things doesn't waste any time bragging—he just goes ahead and does his very best and gets the job done. This kind of person is called an עָנָו (a modest person).

Now if you are an עָנָו , it doesn't mean you can't be proud of doing something well. You should always be pleased with yourself when you do a good job, whether it is singing a song, writing a story, or getting good grades in school. There is a difference between being proud of work well done and bragging about work that never gets done at all. The best way to get your work done is to just go ahead and do it. If you do a good job, you won't have to talk about it. Everyone will be able to see what you did.

But whatever you do, don't brag. Always remember that people who brag are really a drag!

Write עָנָו or בַּעַל גַּאֲוָה next to each description:

1. She talks about being a good singer but she sounds like a rusty hinge. . . . .

2. He says he gets great report cards but he always gives the wrong answers in class . . . .

3. She is always telling her poor friends how much money her family has . . . .

4. He is a very good chess player but he is always teaching others how to play better. . . . .

נַתַּהַר לֵאָה וַתֵּלֶד LEAH BECAME PREGNANT

BERESHIT 29:31–35 ³¹When the Almighty saw that Leah was the less loved, the Almighty let her have a child. But Rachel had none. ³²Leah became pregnant, and she gave birth to a son. She called him Reuven. ³³She gave birth to another son. She named him Shimeon. ³⁴Again she became pregnant, and gave birth to another son. She named him Levi, for she said, "Now my husband will become attached to me, for I have given him three sons." ³⁵Once more she gave birth to a son. She named him Yehudah, for she said, "Now I will thank the Almighty." After this, she stopped giving birth.

BERESHIT 30:1–24 ¹When Rachel saw that she was having no children with Yaakov, she became jealous of her sister. "Give me children or I will die," she said to Yaakov. ²Yaakov became angry with Rachel and answered her, "Can I take the place of God, Who has made you childless?" ³Then Rachel told him, "Here is my maidservant, Bilhah." ⁴She gave him Bilhah, her maidservant, to be his wife. ⁵Bilhah bore Jacob a son. ⁶Rachel named him Dan, for she said, "God has judged in my favor, for God has heard my prayer and given me a son." ⁷Bilhah, Rachel's maidservant, bore Yaakov another son. ⁸Rachel named him Naftali.

⁹When Leah saw that she had stopped having children, she gave her maidservant, Zilpah to Yaakov, to be his wife. ¹⁰Zilpah, Leah's maidservant, bore Yaakov a son. ¹¹Leah named him Gad, for she said, "Luck has come." ¹²Zilpah, Leah's maidservant, bore Yaakov another son. ¹³Leah named him Asher.

¹⁷Now God heard Leah's prayer. She gave birth to Yaakov's fifth son. ¹⁸She named him Yissachar. ¹⁹Then, once again, Leah gave birth. ²⁰She named him Zevulun, for she said, "God has given me a precious gift. I have given my husband six sons." ²¹Afterwards, she gave birth to a daughter, whom she named Dinah.

²²Now God remembered Rachel. God heard her prayer and made it possible for her to bear children. ²³She became pregnant, and gave birth to a son. "God has taken away my disgrace," she said. ²⁴She named him Yoseph for she said, "May the Almighty give me another son."

³ Then the Almighty said to Yaakov, "Return to the land of your ancestors, where you were born."

BERESHIT
31:3

---

18. SHE NAMED HIM YISSACHAR
וַתִּקְרָא שְׁמוֹ יִשָּׂשכָר

Yissachar, in Hebrew, is based on the word *sachar*, which means "rewarded."

Match the Columns

1. Leah's first-born son was
2. Leah's second son was named
3. Leah's third son was named
4. Leah gave thanks for her son
5. Bilhah's son named "He judged" was
6. Bilhah also bore
7. "Luck came" when Zilpah bore
8. Zilpah also gave birth to
9. Leah's fifth son was named
10. "God's precious gift" to Leah was
11. Yaakov's only daughter was
12. Rachel's first born son was

Yehudah
Dan
Shimeon
Reuven
Levi
Gad
Yosef
Yissachar
Zevulun
Asher
Naftali
Dinah

Ideas to Explore

1. Obviously Leah and Rachel considered child-bearing a way to gain Yaakov's love. Is that a crazy notion today? Have times changed?

2. Having children was certainly important to the growth of the Jewish people, but even though Rachel had fewer children than Leah, Yaakov always preferred Rachel. How do you explain this?

3. In this story once again we find wives giving their maid-servants to their husbands as concubines. Do you think these concubines were ignored as people? Give evidence from the story to support your answer.

4. There are two different things Rachel may have meant when she said, "Give me children or I will die." What are they?

We are special because God created us with a brain to think with. We are special, and with our brain we recognize when someone has made our lives happier or more pleasant. We express our appreciation by saying "thank-you," or תּוֹדָה in Hebrew.

1. How did Leah say thank-you to God for sending her a son?

_____

_____

_____

_____

Write a special thank-you message to each of the following people. Thank each person for something they have done to make your life happier or more pleasant.

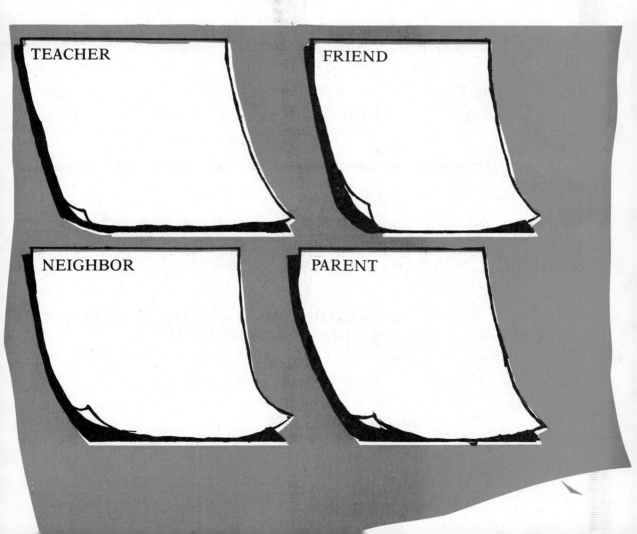

TEACHER

FRIEND

NEIGHBOR

PARENT

הַצִּילֵנִי נָא מִיַּד אָחִי מִיַּד עֵשָׂו

SAVE ME NOW, ALMIGHTY, FROM THE HANDS OF MY BROTHER ESAV

BERESHIT 32:1–13

¹Lavan got up early next morning. He kissed his daughters and grandchildren, bid them good-bye, and started on his journey home. ²Yaakov also went on his way, and God's angels met him. ³When he saw them, Yaakov said, "This is God's camp." And he named the place, "Mahanayim."

⁴Yaakov now sent messengers ahead to his brother, Esav, in Edom, in the land of Seir. ⁵He gave them this message: "To my lord Esav. Your servant Yaakov wishes to inform you that until recently I lived with Lavan.

⁶I am sending you this message, my lord, to

---

3. AND HE NAMED THE PLACE, "MAHANAYIM."

וַיִּקְרָא שֵׁם־הַמָּקוֹם הַהוּא מַחֲנָיִם

מַחֲנָיִם means "two camps": the camp of the angels and the camp of his father-in-law, Lavan.

4. YAAKOV NOW SENT MESSENGERS AHEAD TO HIS BROTHER, ESAV.

וַיִּשְׁלַח יַעֲקֹב מַלְאָכִים לְפָנָיו אֶל־עֵשָׂו אָחִיו

Twenty years had passed since Yaakov fled from Esav's anger. Esav was a warrior and a hunter. Would he take revenge on Yaakov?

Yaakov decides to test Esav and sends him a friendly message.

inform you of our coming, hoping that you will receive us in a friendly manner."

⁷The messengers returned to Yaakov and informed him, "We went to your brother, Esav. He is on his way to meet you, together with 400 men." ⁸Yaakov was terribly frightened. He divided the people with him, as well as the flocks and herds and camels, into two camps. ⁹For he said, "If Esav attacks one camp, perhaps the other will escape."

¹⁰Then Yaakov prayed, "O God of my grandfather Avraham and of my father Yitzchak, O Almighty Who said to me, 'Return to your land and to your family, and I will be good to you,' "I hardly deserve the many kindnesses that You have shown me again and again. For when I crossed the Yarden River, I had no more than a shepherd's stick. And by now I have grown into two camps. ¹²Save me now, Almighty, from the hands of my brother Esav; for I am afraid that he is coming to kill me and all of my family. ¹³For You had promised, 'I will deal generously with you and make your descendants like the sand of the sea, too many to count.' "

---

8. YAAKOV WAS TERRIBLY FRIGHTENED. וַיִּירָא יַעֲקֹב מְאֹד

Yaakov was a brave, strong, and powerful man with many warriors in his camp. Was he really frightened by Esav? Our Rabbis say that Yaakov was frightened that he would have to sin and shed blood.

10. THEN YAAKOV PRAYED. וַיֹּאמֶר יַעֲקֹב

Yaakov does not place all of his eggs in one basket; he adopts three methods of defense. First he prays to God for protection. Second, he sends gifts to Esav as tokens of his good will and love. His third and last strategy is to stand his ground and fight. He tries to settle his problem by peaceful means, but if all else fails, he is ready, willing, and able to fight.

What Do You Think?

1. If you had a friend who was so angry at you that he was likely to hit you the next time you met, what would you do? How would you cool him off?

2. Do you get into arguments or fights pretty often? What ways to avoid fights could you learn from Yaakov?

3. When Yaakov prays to God for help, he first expresses thanks for the kindnesses God has shown him. Before you petition God, what kindnesses could you thank God for?

   A. _____
   B. _____
   C. _____
   D. _____
   E. _____
   _____

4. Yaakov prays, but he also believes that God helps those who help themselves. In the following situations, besides praying, what could you do to help yourself?

   1. You can't seem to understand anything about biology, and a big test is coming up.

   2. You broke your mother's antique vase, and when she finds out your name will be mud.

   3. You're trying out for cheerleaders, and you want to make it more than anything in the world.

Ladders to Success

For seven years Yaakov worked for Rachel's father, Lavan. He had a goal in mind: he wanted to marry the girl he loved—Rachel.

But Lavan fooled him and he married Leah instead. Naturally, Yaakov was angry, but he did not lose sight of his goal. He agreed to work hard for another seven years, and this time Rachel became his wife.

Yaakov had a goal in mind; despite the disappointment, he worked hard and he achieved it.

Life is a series of goals, some small and some large. Each goal we reach helps us climb the ladder of happiness and success. Some goals are very easy and others are more difficult. There may even be goals we can never achieve despite all our hard work. But if you set your eye on a goal and you climb and work hard at it, you will succeed.

Practice your planning skills by completing these ladders to success. Choose two goals you hope to accomplish—one for school and one for home. Start at the bottom of the ladder and list the steps you will need to reach your goal.

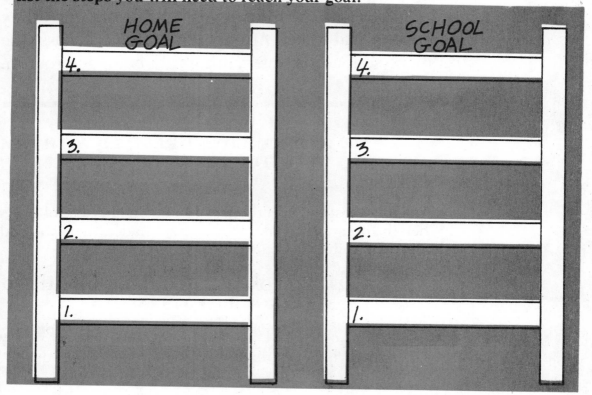

לֹא יֵעָקֵב יֵאָמֵר עוֹד שִׁמְךָ כִּי אִם־יִשְׂרָאֵל

NO LONGER SHALL YOU BE CALLED YAAKOV, BUT YISRAEL

BERESHIT 32:14–33 ¹⁴After staying there for the night, Yaakov selected a present for his brother from what he had with him:

¹⁷He put these into the care of his servants, in separate groups, instructing them, "Move on ahead of me, but keep a space between one group and the next."

²³That same night, he got up, took his two wives, the two maid-servants, and his eleven children, and they crossed the Yabbok. ²⁴After taking them across the stream, he sent across everything that belonged to him.

---

25. AND SOMEONE WRESTLED WITH HIM UNTIL THE BREAK OF DAWN.

וַיֵּאָבֵק אִישׁ עִמּוֹ עַד עֲלוֹת הַשָּׁחַר

Yaakov wrestled with the idea of God and his fear of Esav. When the bout was over and he won, he had faith in God and in his own ability to deal with men such as Esav.

29. NO LONGER SHALL YOU BE CALLED YAAKOV, BUT YISRAEL.

לֹא יֵעָקֵב יֵאָמֵר עוֹד שִׁמְךָ כִּי אִם־יִשְׂרָאֵל

The name Yisrael is made up of two Hebrew words: שַׂר ("prince") and אֵל ("God"). It means "prince of God."

²⁵But Yaakov himself remained behind, all alone, and someone wrestled with him until the break of dawn. ²⁶When the opponent saw that he could not win against Yaakov, he struck Yaakov's hip-socket, so that it became strained.

²⁷"Let me go," the opponent pleaded, "for it is dawn." But Yaakov answered him, "I will not let you go until you bless me." ²⁸He then asked Yaakov, "What is your name?" And Yaakov told him. ²⁹"Well, then," he said, "no longer shall you be called Yaakov, but Yisrael. For you are now Prince of God who has had victory over men!" ³⁰And Yaakov asked, "What is your name?" He answered, "You must not ask that." But he blessed Yaakov there.

³¹Yaakov named the place "Peniel," saying, "I have seen God face to face, yet I have lived." ³²As he left Peniel, the sun began to rise. He limped now because of his hip. ³³That is why, to this day, the children of Yisrael do not eat of the thigh-vein which attaches to the hip.

---

31. NAMED THE PLACE "PENIEL."

וַיִּקְרָא יַעֲקֹב שֵׁם הַמָּקוֹם פְּנִיאֵל

פְּנִיאֵל is made up of two Hebrew words: פְּנֵי ("face of") and אֵל ("God"). It means "face of God."

138

Answer " כֵּן " or " לֹא "

1. Yaakov stayed with his family during the entire trip. _____

2. Yaakov slept peacefully. _____

3. Someone wrestled with Yaakov all night. _____

4. Yaakov won the fight. _____

5. Yaakov was not injured. _____

Answer the Questions

1. What did Yaakov's opponent do when he saw that he could not win the fight?

2. What did Yaakov ask for before he would release his opponent?

3. What was Yaakov's new name?

4. What did Yaakov name the place where he wrestled?

5. Why don't we eat the part of an animal that contains the thigh-vein?

Ideas to Explore

1. Why do you think that Yaakov sent the others on ahead and remained by himself all night?

2. With whom did Yaakov wrestle? An angel? Himself?

3. Why did Yaakov's opponent insist that he must leave at dawn? So that Yaakov couldn't see his face? Because he was really a dream opponent?

4. Yaakov could have asked for anything, but once again he asked for a blessing. Why do you think he did?

5. Why do you think Yaakov was given a new name?

6. What experiences helped Yaakov become a better person?

7. Have you ever had an experience that helped you "grow up"?

The Children of Yisrael בְּנֵי יִשְׂרָאֵל

This is the first time that the name יִשְׂרָאֵל (Israel) appears in the Torah. Since Yaakov's twelve sons became the founders and leaders of the twelve tribes, they came to be called the twelve tribes of יִשְׂרָאֵל.

Outside the Torah, the name יִשְׂרָאֵל is not found on many of the documents, walls, or stones that archaeologists have uncovered. The earliest record of the name יִשְׂרָאֵל is on a victory monument of the Pharaoh Merneptah, who lived about two or three hundred years after Yaakov. There the name was found in the ancient Egyptian picture-writing (hieroglyphics).

Avraham, Yitzchak, and Yaakov (יִשְׂרָאֵל) were all Patriarchs. Yet the Jews are called the Children of יִשְׂרָאֵל. Why not "Children of Avraham" or "Children of Yaakov"?

Our Rabbis point out that Avraham was the father of two nations, the Children of יִשְׂרָאֵל and the Yishmaelites. The Yishmaelites were enemies of the Children of יִשְׂרָאֵל.

Yitzchak was also the father of two nations, the Children of Yisrael and the Edomites. The Edomites were also enemies of the Children of יִשְׂרָאֵל and were always at war with them.

However, יִשְׂרָאֵל had twelve sons—and all of them were Yisraelites.

Teshuvah

Through the long dark night, Yaakov wrestles with his fears of his brother Esav and with his conscience, which has haunted him these past twenty years. As soon as the sun begins to rise, the wrestler disappears and a new life dawns for Yaakov. His past evaporates into the night and his fears of Esav disappear.

Yaakov is back on the right track — he is now a בַּעַל תְּשׁוּבָה (a "master of repentance"). In recognition of his new character and new life, his old name is discarded and he is given the new name of Yisrael.

Human beings can improve their own lives by doing תְּשׁוּבָה. Sins are just temporary obstacles, and we can all improve our conduct by doing תְּשׁוּבָה.

One of the eighteen benedictions of the עֲמִידָה prayer, which is recited three times daily, deals with the theme of תְּשׁוּבָה.

וַיָּרץ עֵשָׂו לִקְרָאתוֹ ESAV RAN TO GREET HIM

BERESHIT
33:1–17
[1]Yaakov looked up and saw Esav coming with his 400 men. He now divided his children among Leah, Rachel, and the two maid-servants. [2]He put the maid-servants and their children in front, Leah and her children next, and Rachel with Yosef last. [3]He himself went ahead of them all. As he approached his brother, he bowed low before him, seven times.

[4]Esav ran to greet him. He embraced him affectionately and kissed him. And both of them cried. [5]When Esav looked around and saw the women and children, he asked, "Who are these people with you?" Yaakov answered, "These are the children that God has blessed me with."

---

3. HE HIMSELF WENT AHEAD OF THEM ALL.
וְהוּא עָבַר לִפְנֵיהֶם

Yaakov was afraid that Esav still hated him and would attack him and his family. So Yaakov went ahead to meet his brother and ask for his forgiveness. Should he fail, Yaakov is prepared to sacrifice himself and fight so that his wives and his children can escape.

4. ESAV RAN TO GREET HIM.   וַיָּרץ עֵשָׂו לִקְרָאתוֹ

This is a great surprise. After all of Yaakov's fear and the preparations he had made for a possible attack, Esav not only welcomes him but runs to greet him. Yaahov's fear led him to imagine danger. His wrestling with the angel had given him back his courage. Now he comes face-to-face with what he fears—and like a bad dream, it disappears.

⁸"And what about all the flocks and herds that I met along the way?" Esav asked. "For you. To win your favor," Yaakov answered. ⁹"But I have plenty, my brother!" Esav said. "Keep it for yourself." ¹⁰"No, I beg you. Do me the favor of accepting the gift. For seeing your kind face is like coming into God's presence. ¹⁶That same day, Esav started back on his way to Seir. ¹⁷Yaakov moved on to Succoth, where he built a house for himself and sheds for his flocks and herds. For this reason was the place named, "Succoth."

---

10. FOR SEEING YOUR KIND FACE IS LIKE COMING INTO GOD'S PRESENCE.

כִּי עַל־כֵּן רָאִיתִי פָנֶיךָ כִּרְאֹת פְּנֵי אֱלֹהִים

Your kind face and friendly behavior mean that you have forgiven me. I have been in God's presence, and God also has forgiven me.

17. YAAKOV MOVED ON TO SUCCOTH.

וְיַעֲקֹב נָסַע סֻכֹּתָה

The city of Succoth, which has the same name as the fall festival, is mentioned several times in the Bible. Succoth was situated in the Yarden plain and was in a position to control the valley between two important rivers, the Yarden and the Yabbok.

About 4,000 years ago, Yaakov built "Succoth" for his family after his reconciliation with his brother Esav.

The area around Succoth was noted for its high-quality clay. Thousands of pieces of pottery dating back to Bible times have been found in this area.

The clay from Succoth was also used to make molds for casting copper. It was in this area that the fine copper utensils and adornments for Solomon's Temple were cast.

Answer the Questions

1. Did Esav accept Yaakov's gifts?
2. Where did Esav go after their meeting?
3. Where did Yaakov settle?
4. Why was the place named Succoth?

Ideas to Explore

1. What were the maid-servants to Yaakov?
2. Why do you think that Yaakov bowed before his brother Esav?
3. Do you think that Esav had really intended to fight Yaakov? Do you think that Yaakov's gifts and family helped to make peace?
4. When Esav accepted Yaakov's gifts, was that a way of saying, "Okay, I forgive you"?
5. Why do you think that Esav hurried off that same day, after not seeing his brother so many years? Were they good friends or not?

Goals and Cooperation

Yaakov's goal was to make peace with his brother Esav. He worked at achieving the goal and he succeeded.

A goal is something a person wants and tries to reach. When you are hungry, you try to get food. At that moment, your goal is getting food. Learning to play the guitar is another kind of goal. Some people want to learn. They practice many hours. Their goal is learning to play the guitar.

Some goals are shared by several people. You and your friends might want to have a party together. Planning the party would be a shared goal.

We sometimes try to get what we want by working with others. This is called cooperation. Cooperation happens when people work together to reach a goal all of them share.

Write a personal goal for today.

List the things you will have to do to reach the goal.

Write a goal for tomorrow.

Think back over yesterday. Write a goal you achieved that needed the cooperation of others.

NOW THE SONS OF YAAKOV WERE TWELVE

וַיִּהְיוּ בְנֵי־יַעֲקֹב שְׁנֵים עָשָׂר

**BERESHIT
35:16–29** ¹⁶Then they left Beth-El and headed toward Efrath. When still some distance from Efrath, Rachel gave birth to a child with difficulty. ¹⁷While Rachel was giving birth, the midwife said to her, "Have no fear. You have another son." ¹⁸With her last breath—for she was dying—she named him Ben-oni. But his father called him Binyamin. ¹⁹Rachel died and was buried on the road to Efrath, now Bethlehem. ²⁰Yaakov set up a

---

18. SHE NAMED HIM BEN-ONİ.

וַתִּקְרָא שְׁמוֹ בֶּן עוֹנִי

As Rachel lay dying with her last breath, she named her son "בֶּן עוֹנִי," meaning "son of my sorrow." Yaakov changed the name to "Binyamin," meaning "the son of my right hand."

Yaakov loved Rachel very much. She was his "right hand." In the doing of מִצְווֹת she was his right hand, and also in teaching the idol-worshippers about the Supreme Being.

Some commentators say that, Binyamin is for "son of days" meaning "son of his old age".

19. RACHEL DIED AND WAS BURIED ON THE ROAD TO EFRATH, NOW BETHLEHEM.

וַתָּמָת רָחֵל וַתִּקָּבֵר בְּדֶרֶךְ אֶפְרָתָה הוּא בֵּית לָחֶם

The domed structure known to millions of Jews as the Tomb of Rachel, the favorite wife of Yaakov, is situated seven miles from Jerusalem in Bethlehem. This monument was erected by the Crusaders in the twelfth century. The well-known philanthropist, Sir Moses Montefiore, bought the Tomb in 1841 and reconstructed it for worshipping Jews. He also added a small hall with a prayer corner for Moslems, who also consider Rachel a sacred person.

monument over her grave. It is the same monument that marks her grave to this day. ²¹Then Yisrael moved on and pitched his tent beyond Migdal-eder.

²²While Yisrael was living in that region, Reuven took Bilhah, his father's maid-servant for himself. And Yisrael heard about it.

²³Now the sons of Yaakov were twelve. The sons of Leah: Reuven, Yaakov's first-born, Shimeon, Levi, Yehudah, Yissachar, Zevulun.

²⁴The sons of Rachel: Yoseph, Binyamin.

²⁵The sons of Bilhah, Rachel's maid-servant: Dan, Naftali.

²⁶The sons of Zilpah, Leah's maid-servant: Gad, Asher. These were the sons of Yaakov who were born to him in Paddan-aram.

²⁷Now Yaakov came home to his father, Yitzchak, at Mamre, in Kiryath-arba, now Hebron, where Avraham and Yitzchak had lived. ²⁸Yitzchak was 180 years old. ²⁹Yitzchak died among his family at a ripe old age, and he was buried by his sons, Esav and Yaakov.

---

20. YAAKOV SET UP A MONUMENT OVER HER GRAVE.

וַיַּצֵּב יַעֲקֹב מַצֵּבָה עַל־קְבֻרָתָהּ

מַצֵּבָה is the Hebrew word for a grave monument or tombstone. Today, it is customary for Jews to set a מַצֵּבָה at the head of the grave. Its purpose is to keep the memory of the dead alive as well as to identify the grave. The usual practice is to erect a מַצֵּבָה one year after the death. The stone is covered with a veil. A service is conducted by the family and the veil is removed. This service is called an unveiling.

Match the Columns

1. Leah's sons were
2. Rachel's sons were
3. Bilhah's sons were
4. Zilpah's sons were

Yosef, Binyamin

Gad, Asher

Dan, Naftali

Reuven, Shimeon, Levi, Yehudah, Yissachar, Zevulun

Answer the Questions

1. What happened to Rachel on the road to Ephrath?
2. What did she name her son?
3. What did Yaakov call him?
4. What is the name of the place where Rachel died, and a monument marks her grave?
5. How old was Yitzchak when he died?

Ideas to Explore

1. Why did Yaakov stay away from Canaan for so long?
2. Why do you think he returned?
3. When Yitzchak died, he was buried by both his sons—Esav and Yaakov. What does this tell you about the relationship between the two?

It's a Mitzvah to Share.

A mitzvah, or commandment, is something that God wants us to do. It brings the great ideas of our religion into our everyday lives. At the same time, a mitzvah is something that helps us, that makes us happier or healthier or wiser or better people.

It is a mitzvah to share with others and to help them. When we share and help, we are doing something God wants us to do. Then we are good and we feel good.

There are many, many mitzvot, or commandments, in our religion. There are mitzvot about foods and holidays and ceremonies and about honoring our parents and about honesty and about how to treat other people, and about prayer.

Mitzvot are our duty and our privilege too. They help us live in a holy way.

Let's follow some mitzvot through a chain.

Try to think of ways in which the following mitzvah might lead to other mitzvot.

Situation One:

You are playing in the street, suddenly you see someone who seems sick.

You run over and help the person.

What other mitzvot may this lead to in the future?

_____

_____

_____

Situation Two:

A foreign student is in your class. She is having trouble with her schoolwork. You offer to help her after school.

What other mitzvot may result from this one mitzvah?

_____

וְיִשְׂרָאֵל אָהַב אֶת־יוֹסֵף
YISRAEL LOVED YOSEPH

¹Yaakov was now settled in the land of Canaan, where his father had lived. ²The further events in his life follow.

Yoseph was seventeen years old. Along with his half-brothers, the sons of his father's wives Bilhah and Zilpah, he tended the flocks. But he tattled about his brothers to his father. ³Now Yisrael loved Yoseph more than any of his other sons, because Yoseph was born to him in his old age. So he made him a tunic of many colors. ⁴When his brothers saw that their father loved him best among all of them, they hated him and could not say a kind word to him. ◉

---

2 YOSEPH   יוֹסֵף

Yoseph was considered Yaakov's most important descendant. His mother, Rachel, was Yaakov's true love, and Yaakov had only to look upon Yoseph's face to be reminded of his beloved Rachel.

2. BUT HE TATTLED ABOUT HIS BROTHERS TO HIS FATHER.
וַיָּבֵא יוֹסֵף אֶת־דִּבָּתָם רָעָה אֶל־אֲבִיהֶם

Yoseph's mother, Rachel, had died. So Yoseph attached himself to the families of Bilhah and Zilpah. Yoseph would report to Yaakov what the boys were doing, which, naturally, made them angry.

3. SO HE MADE HIM A TUNIC OF MANY COLORS.
וְעָשָׂה לוֹ כְּתֹנֶת פַּסִּים

Yaakov was showing favoritism to Yoseph over all his brothers, which was an unwise thing to do. The tunic which Yaakov gave Yoseph was a long-sleeved garment which reached down to the ankles.

⁵One time, Yoseph had a dream, which he told to his brothers. This made them hate him even more. ⁶"Listen to the dream I had!" he said to them. ⁷"We were out in the field binding sheaves, when suddenly my sheaf stood up, and your sheaves formed a circle around my sheaf and bowed down to it." ⁸ His brothers asked him, "So you're going to be king over us? You think that you will rule us!" And they hated him even more for his talk about his dreams. ⁹Then he had a second dream and told it to his brothers. "Look, I had another dream. The sun, the moon, and eleven stars were bowing down to me!" ¹⁰When he told it to his father and his brothers, his father criticized him, "What kind of dream is this that you have had?" he asked. "Do you really expect that I and your mother and your brothers shall come bowing before you?" ¹¹His brothers were jealous of him. But his father thought about it.

---

9. THE SUN, THE MOON, AND ELEVEN STARS WERE BOWING DOWN TO ME.

וְהִנֵּה הַשֶּׁמֶשׁ וְהַיָּרֵחַ וְאַחַד עָשָׂר כּוֹכָבִים מִשְׁתַּחֲוִים לִי

In the first dream, Yoseph's brothers were bowing before him. Now, in the second dream, his father and mother, along with his brothers, were doing it.

11. HIS BROTHERS WERE JEALOUS OF HIM, BUT HIS FATHER THOUGHT ABOUT IT.

וַיְקַנְאוּ־בוֹ אֶחָיו וְאָבִיו שָׁמַר אֶת הַדָּבָר

Yoseph's brothers resented him more than ever. But Yaakov wondered whether these dreams might be fulfilled someday.

Complete the Sentences

1. Yaakov settled in the land of _____.
2. Yisrael loved _____ more than his other sons.
3. Yoseph tattled about his brothers to his _____.
4. The sun, moon, and _____ bowed down to me.
5. Yoseph was a _____.

Yoseph, dreamer, Canaan, stars, father.

What Do You Think?

1. Why do you think Yaakov loved Joseph more than any of his other sons?
2. Why were the brothers angry at Yoseph?
3. How did Yaakov show his love for Yoseph?
4. How did the brothers interpret the first dream?
5. How did Yaakov interpret the second dream?
6. In sentence 10, we find the phrase, "but his father thought about it." Do you think Yaakov believed Yoseph's second dream? Why?

Answer the Questions

1. Where did Yaakov settle?
2. Who was a tattletale?
3. Which son was Yisrael's favorite?
4. How did Yisrael show his love for Yoseph?
5. How many dreams did Yoseph have?
6. What was the meaning of the eleven stars?
7. Who were the sun and moon supposed to be?

Don't Brag—It's A Drag

Yoseph was a handsome young man with special intelligence. He boasted about his special abilities and made sure everyone knew about it.

Yoseph was Yaakov's favorite son, and gave Yaakov a coat with many colors. Unfortunately, this gift only increased his unpopularity, and the boasting became more frequent.

It's okay to be proud of your abilities, but bragging will only make your friends and family angry and jealous.

Of course, like Yoseph, you are a very special person. Just do yourself a little favor.

Keep it to yourself.

Don't brag—it's a drag.

1. Why do some people have to brag to feel important?
2. Do you feel important when you brag?
3. What do you think when you hear someone bragging?

הִנֵּה בַּעַל הַחֲלֹמוֹת הַלָּזֶה בָּא

HERE COMES THE DREAMER

BERESHIT 37:13–36

¹³Yisrael said to Yoseph, "Your brothers are grazing the flocks around Shechem. I want you to go over to see them." "I am ready," he answered. ¹⁴"Go now. See how your brothers and their flocks are doing, and bring back word to me."

¹⁸Then they saw him from the distance, and before he came close to them they decided to kill him. ¹⁹"Here comes that dreamer!" they said to each other. ²⁰"Let's kill him and toss him into one of the pits. We'll say, 'A wild animal has eaten him.' Then we'll see what becomes of his dreams."

²¹But when Reuven heard this, he tried to rescue him from them. "We must not kill him," he said. ²²"Do not shed any blood!" Reuven told them. "Just throw him into a pit, out there in the desert, but don't lay a hand on him." He intended to save him from their hands and get him back to his father. ²³So when Yoseph reached his brothers, they

---

13. "I AM READY," HE ANSWERED.

וַיֹּאמֶר לוֹ הִנֵּנִי

Yoseph knew well that his brothers hated him. Yet he eagerly agreed to visit them, for he loved his father and wished to do his bidding.

22. DO NOT SHED ANY BLOOD!

אַל־תִּשְׁפְּכוּ־דָם

Reuven argued: "Why should we murder our brother with our own hands? Let us throw him into this pit. The area is deserted, and he will starve to death."

stripped him of the colorful tunic which he was wearing. ²⁴They picked him up and threw him into an empty pit that was dry.

²⁵They now sat down to eat. Suddenly, they saw a caravan of Yishmaelites coming from Gilead, their camels loaded· with spices, balm, and gum. They were on their way down to Egypt. They sold him to the Yishmaelites for twenty pieces of silver, and they took Yoseph along with them to Egypt.

³¹Then the brothers killed a goat and dipped the tunic in the blood. ³²They sent someone with the tunic of many colors to their father, along with the message, "We have found this. Is it your son's tunic?" ³³He recognized it and said, "It is my son's tunic! A wild animal has devoured him! Yoseph has been destroyed!" ³⁴Then Yaakov tore his clothes, put on sackcloth, and mourned for his son many weeks.

³⁶Meanwhile, in Egypt, the traders sold Yoseph to Potiphar, one of Pharaoh's officers. He was captain of the guard and the head executioner.

---

23. AND THEY STRIPPED HIM OF THE COLORFUL TUNIC.

וַיַּפְשִׁיטוּ אֶת־יוֹסֵף אֶת־כֻּתָּנְתּוֹ אֶת־כְּתֹנֶת הַפַּסִּים

Before the brothers delivered Yoseph up to what they felt would be certain death, they stripped him of the symbol of his father's love and of their jealousy—the coat of many colors.

32. THEY SENT SOMEONE WITH THE TUNIC OF MANY COLORS TO THEIR FATHER.

וַיְשַׁלְּחוּ אֶת־כְּתֹנֶת הַפַּסִּים וַיָּבִיאוּ אֶל־אֲבִיהֶם

Yoseph's brothers were afraid to come to their father. They sent the tunic with a messenger.

34. THEN YAAKOV TORE HIS CLOTHES, PUT ON SACKCLOTH, AND MOURNED FOR HIS SON MANY WEEKS.

וַיִּקְרַע יַעֲקֹב שִׂמְלֹתָיו וַיָּשֶׂם שַׂק בְּמָתְנָיו וַיִּתְאַבֵּל עַל־בְּנוֹ יָמִים רַבִּים

In the Biblical period, the wearing of sackcloth and sprinkling ashes on the head expressed mourning for the dead. The sackcloth was a rough cloth which was made of goat's hair.

Match the Columns

Potiphar	tunic
Yishmaelites	city
colorful	Egyptian
twenty pieces	mourning
sack cloth	caravan
Shechem	silver

What Do You Think?

1. Was it a good idea for Yisrael to send Yoseph to find his brothers? Why not?

2. Why didn't the brothers themselves bring the bloody tunic to Yisrael?

3. Was Yaakov aware that the brothers hated Yoseph?

Answer the Questions

1. Where were the brothers grazing their flocks?
2. Who tried to save Yoseph?
3. Where did the brothers throw Yoseph?
4. To whom did the brothers sell Yoseph?
5. Who bought Yoseph from the traders?

Follow-the-Leader

All of the brothers except Reuven decided to follow the leader and sell Yoseph. Reuven wanted to return when the brothers were gone and free Yoseph. The Midrash says that Shimeon was the leader and the rest of the brothers followed him.

We are all responsible for our own actions and do not have to follow someone else's lead. Each and everyone of us can say "no!"

Lots of times in our lives, just like Yoseph's brothers, we are asked to play follow-the-leader. Some times we are asked to follow even when it is not a game.

What would you choose to do in each of these situations: follow or not follow?

"Let's sneak into the house and take some of the cookies my mom is saving!" _____

_____

_____

An adult says to a group of children, "Lie about your age and you will be able to buy a cheaper ticket." _____

_____

_____

Your friend shows you tomorrow's test. He says, "I'll let you study the exam." _____

_____

_____

Your parents are out of the house running some errands. Your brother says, "Let's clean up the kitchen." _____

_____

_____

The rabbi asks you and your group to visit an old age home. You think this is boring and refuse to go. _____

_____

_____

וַיּוֹסֵף הוּרַד מִצְרָיְמָה

WHEN YOSEPH WAS BROUGHT DOWN TO EGYPT

BERESHIT
39:1–20

¹When Yoseph was brought down to Egypt by the Yishmaelites, he was bought from them by Potiphar, an important official on Pharaoh's staff. ³His master saw that the Lord blessed Yoseph in everything that he did. ⁴He was very much impressed by Yoseph, and promoted him to be the manager of his entire estate

⁷After a time, Potiphar's wife took a great liking for Yoseph, and she said, "Come to me." ⁸But he refused. ¹¹Then one day, Yoseph went into the house to go about his work and none of the servants were around at the time. ¹²She took hold of his coat and said, "Come to me." Yoseph tore away. As he did so, his coat came off and it remained in her hands. He ran from the house.

---

1. YOSEPH WAS BROUGHT DOWN TO EGYPT.

וַיּוֹסֵף הוּרַד מִצְרָיְמָה

Since Yisrael is always considered "above" all other lands, the Torah says that Yoseph was "brought **down**" to the land of Egypt.

3. HIS MASTER SAW THAT THE LORD BLESSED YOSEPH

וַיְהִי יְהֹוָה אֶת־יוֹסֵף וַיְהִי אִישׁ מַצְלִיחַ

According to the Rabbis, the name of God was always on his lips in prayer and thanksgiving.

¹⁶She kept his coat beside her until her husband came home. ¹⁷Then she told him the same story. "That Hebrew slave you brought into our house came in and insulted me."

¹⁹When the master heard his wife's story about what the Hebrew slave had done, he became furious. ²⁰So Yoseph's master took him and threw him into prison, where the king's prisoners were kept.

---

3. IN EVERYTHING THAT HE DID.

וְכֹל אֲשֶׁר הוּא עֹשֶׂה יְהוָה מַצְלִיחַ בְּיָדוֹ

Originally sold as a slave, Yoseph had become administrator of his master's estate and his close adviser.

20. SO YOSEPH'S MASTER TOOK HIM AND THREW HIM INTO PRISON.

וַיִּקַּח אֲדֹנֵי יוֹסֵף אֹתוֹ וַיִּתְּנֵהוּ אֶל־בֵּית הַסֹּהַר

Potiphar must have had some doubt about the charge against Yoseph. Otherwise, he would have had Yoseph put to death instead of imprisoning him.

Complete the Sentences

1. The _____ bought Yoseph from the brothers.
2. Potiphar was an important official on _____ staff.
3. Potiphar promoted _____ to be the manager of his estate.
4. Potiphar's _____ took a liking to Yoseph.
5. Yoseph's master threw him into _____.

Pharaoh's, wife, prison, Yishmaelites, Yoseph

Answer the Questions

1. Who brought Yoseph to Egypt?
2. Who bought Yoseph as a slave?
3. Who took a liking to Yoseph?
4. Who lied to Potiphar about Yoseph?

What Do You Think?

1. Why was Yoseph promoted to a managerial position?
2. What is meant by the phrase "the Lord blessed Yoseph in everything he did"?
3. Why did Potiphar's wife lie to her husband?
4. Did Potiphar really believe his wife? Why not?
5. Why didn't Potiphar condemn Yoseph to death?

Yoseph Grows Up

Parents and teachers will occasionally say to us, impatiently: "Come on, it's time to grow up" They mean by that challenge that we've lived long enough to be more mature, to act in keeping with our age.

Yoseph was challenged by his early experiences in Egypt to grow up fast. No more was there that favoritism and sheltering to which he was accustomed at home. He was on his own, and he had to sink or swim.

The first challenge came to him as a slave in Potiphar's house. He was doing well in growing up to the responsibility of work. But Potiphar's wife, angry with him and vengeful, charged him with wrongdoing. Off to prison he went, although on false charges. It should have broken his spirit but it did not. He was growing up fast to the challenges of life. Very soon, his ability was recognized and Yoseph was appointed a prison trustee. By now he had learned from the bitter experience with his brothers to play fair with people. The warden had confidence in him. Yoseph's fellow prisoners liked him. He was maturing.

1. Define and explain the word "mature."
2. What experiences have helped you grow up?
3. Can you remember an experience that "threw you for a loop"?
4. How do you beat the blues and the blahs?
5. Did anyone help you get out of the blues and the blahs?

חֲלוֹם חָלַמְנוּ

WE EACH HAD A DREAM

BERESHIT
40:1–22 ¹Some time later, his Highness the King of Egypt was somehow insulted by his chief cup-bearer and chief baker. ²Pharaoh was therefore angry with these officials. ³He had them jailed by the warden in the same prison where Yoseph was.

⁵One night during their imprisonment, both the cup-bearer and the baker had each a dream. Each dream had its own meaning. ⁶When Yoseph came to them in the morning, he saw that they were depressed. ⁷So he asked these officials of Pharaoh who were imprisoned with him, ''Why such sad looks on your faces?'' ⁸And they answered, ''We each had a dream, but there is no one around to tell us what they mean.

---

1. THE CHIEF BAKER. הָאֹפֶה

The chief baker was jailed because a pebble had been found in the bread baked for the king's table. The chief butler was imprisoned because a fly had been found in the wine he had poured for the king.

3. WHEN YOSEPH CAME TO THEM.

וַיָּבֹא אֲלֵיהֶם יוֹסֵף

The two new prisoners were noblemen, and so a servant was assigned them even in prison. God works in mysterious ways. The inmate chosen to be their servant was none other than Yoseph.

⁹Then the chief cup-bearer told Yoseph his dream. ¹²Yoseph said to him, "This is what it means. The three branches are three days. ¹³Within three days, Pharaoh will pardon you and return you to your office. You will be his cup-bearer, handing the cup to Pharaoh, as you did in the past. ¹⁴Now do me a favor and think of me when all is well with you again. Mention me to Pharaoh, and try to free me from this place."

¹⁶When the chief baker saw how well Yoseph had interpreted the first dream, he told his dream to him: "Concerning my dream, there were three wicker baskets on my head. ¹⁷In the top basket there were all kinds of baked goods for Pharaoh, but the birds ate it out of the basket on my head." ¹⁸Yoseph answered, "This is the meaning. The three baskets are three days. ¹⁹Within three days Pharaoh will cut off your head and have you hanging from a tree. And the birds will pick off your flesh."

²⁰On the third day, which happened to be Pharaoh's birthday, he made a party for all of his servants. At that time he sent for the chief cup-bearer and the chief baker. ²¹He returned the chief cup-bearer to his assignment, so that he again handed the cup to Pharaoh. ²²But the chief baker was hanged, as Yoseph had predicted.

---

8. WE EACH HAD A DREAM, BUT THERE IS NO ONE AROUND TO TELL US WHAT THEY MEAN.

חֲלוֹם חָלַמְנוּ וּפֹתֵר אֵין אֹתוֹ

Whenever they had dreamed before, they had gone to their personal dream-interpreter for an explanation. But now, as prisoners, whom did they have to do it for them? Then Yoseph offers his help.

20. PHARAOH'S BIRTHDAY.

יוֹם הֻלֶּדֶת אֶת־פַּרְעֹה

On his birthday the Egyptian ruler would pardon some prisoners.

Complete the Sentences

1. The three branches are _____ days.
2. Mention me to _____ and try to free me.
3. Three wicker _____ on my head.
4. Within three days Pharaoh will cut off your _____.
5. He returned the _____ to his assignment.

Pharaoh, baskets, cup-bearer, head, three

Answer the Questions

1. Who insulted the King of Egypt?
2. Who in the Egyptian prison had a dream?
3. According to Yoseph what was the meaning of the 3 branches?
4. Who ate the baked goods in the wicker baskets?
5. What happened to the chief baker?

What Do You Think?

1. Why was the Pharaoh angry at the cup-bearer?
2. Why was the Pharaoh angry at the chief baker?
3. Why were the two prisoners sad?
4. Was the cup-bearer happy with Yoseph's explanation?
5. What makes you think that Yoseph really believed his own explanation?

Dreams

The scientists today who are most concerned with dreams are doctors called psychiatrists. They say that dreams tell us about our deepest feelings, usually wishes or fears. Because we usually try to get what we wish for, our dreams do sometimes seem to come true. But as anyone who has dreamed knows, dreams are not always easy to understand. They seem to be in code. They are full of symbols—things which stand for something else, like Yoseph's stars or Pharaoh's cows. Psychiatrists try to help people decode their dreams. In this sense Yoseph turns out to be a very good psychiatrist.

1. Do you dream?
2. Do you remember your dreams?
3. What do you dream about?
4. What is a daydream?
5. Do you daydream?
6. When do you usually daydream?
7. Where do you usually daydream?
8. What do you daydream about?
9. Do daydreams interfere with your schoolwork?

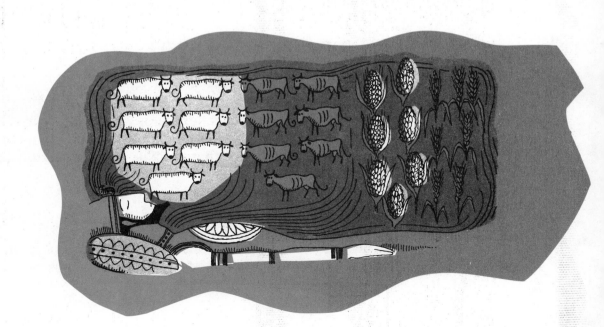

וּפַרְעֹה חֹלֵם

PHARAOH HAD A DREAM

BERESHIT
41:1-12

¹Two years later, Pharaoh had a dream. He was standing by the Nile. ²Suddenly, seven sleek, fat cows came up out of the river and grazed in the reed-grass. ³Behind them, seven other cows, ugly and skinny, came up out of the Nile and stood on the bank of the river beside the fat ones. ⁴And the ugly, skinny cows ate up the seven sleek, fat cows. Then Pharaoh awoke.

⁵But he fell asleep again and had a second dream. Seven ears of grain, fat and solid, were growing on a single stalk. ⁶Immediately after them, seven more ears, shriveled and scorched by the east wind. ⁷And the thin ears swallowed up the seven fat and solid ears. Then Pharaoh awoke to find it was all a dream!

---

1. TWO YEARS LATER. וַיְהִי מִקֵּץ שְׁנָתַיִם יָמִים

Two years after the incident with the cup-bearer and the baker.

4. SUDDENLY, SEVEN SLEEK, FAT COWS CAME UP OUT OF THE RIVER.
וְהִנֵּה מִן־הַיְאֹר עֹלֹת שֶׁבַע פָּרוֹת יְפוֹת מַרְאֶה

The Nile is Egypt's only source of water, and it irrigates all the fields of the country. The fine cows and grain rising from the river symbolize that the Nile gives life to the land and food to the people.

6. SCORCHED BY THE EAST WIND.
קָדִים צֹמְחוֹת אַחֲרֵיהֶן

The east wind is the hot *chamsin* that can last for days and parches the vegetation. It brings with it sandstorms.

⁸Next morning, his spirit disturbed, he sent for all the magicians and wise men of Egypt. Pharaoh told them his dreams, but not one could interpret them for Pharaoh. ⁹Then the chief cup-bearer spoke up and said to Pharaoh, "Today I must recall my wrongs. ¹⁰Once, when Pharaoh was angry with his servants, he put me and the chief baker into jail, under the custody of the warden.

¹²"With us there was a Hebrew youth who was the warden's servant. When we told him our dreams, he interpreted them for us. He told us the meaning of each of our dreams."

---

8. BUT NOT ONE COULD INTERPRET THEM FOR PHARAOH. וְאֵין־פּוֹתֵר אוֹתָם לְפַרְעֹה

Many interpretations were suggested to Pharaoh, but none of the magicians understood the significance of the dreams for the whole country.

12. WITH US THERE WAS A HEBREW YOUTH WHO WAS THE WARDEN'S SERVANT. וְשָׁם אִתָּנוּ נַעַר עִבְרִי עֶבֶד לְשַׂר הַטַּבָּחִים

Even when the chief butler finally did mention Yoseph to Pharaoh, he belittled him—calling him "a boy" and "a slave."

Complete the Sentences

1. The seven ugly cows ate up the _____ sleek, fat cows.

2. The thin ears swallowed up the seven _____ ears.

3. With us there was a _____ youth, who was the warden's servant.

4. He told us the _____ of each of our dreams.

5. Two years later _____ had a dream.

Pharaoh, Hebrew, seven, fat and solid, meaning

Answer the Questions

1. Who dreamed of seven fat and seven thin cows?

2. Which cows ate up the fat cows?

3. Who swallowed the fat and solid ears of corn?

4. How many dreams did Pharaoh have?

5. Were the wise men of Egypt able to interpret the two dreams?

What Do You Think?

1. Did the Egyptian believe in dreams coming true?

2. Why were the cows near the river.

3. Why was the corn planted near the river?

4. If the cows were skinny, and the corn was shriveled, what does that tell you about the water and the grass?

5. What could cause the corn to be thin?

6. If the corn was thin, would the cows be thin or fat?

Archeology of the Humash

Besides underground wells and springs a chief source of water in Biblical lands was the rivers. This is true even today. The Nile in Egypt and the Tigris and Euphrates in Babylonia are the most important rivers in the area. The crops each year depended on these rivers for water. Each year the river would overflow its banks. The floodwaters irrigated the fields and left a valuable layer of fresh topsoil.

In Israel, however, one of the most important sources of water was rain. Famine would follow if there was not enough rain for one or two seasons in a row. Thus there was always the problem of how to save the rain, which often came all at once and not spread over the whole year. In the Negev, the rain naturally and quickly flowed into dry river beds called wadis, which then carried the water down to the Dead Sea, where it was lost in all that salty water.

One ancient group of people who were very good at saving rain water was the Nabateans.

The Nabateans הַנַּבָּטִים

For seventeen hundred years, the Negev lay idle and neglected, a playground for fierce desert winds and sun. Then the Nabateans arrived. A desert people, the Nabateans knew how to survive in the Negev. They knew how to trap and save water. They built dams that stored water during the rainy season for use in dry times. The Nabateans were excellent farmers and grew enough food for themselves as well as for the passing caravans.

The Nabateans also became very successful traders. They opened ports at Gaza and Eilat. From there they traded with India, Arabia, and Greece. Archaeologists have found traces of over three hundred Nabatean villages and believe that at one time there were more than 100,000 of these industrious desert farmers living in the Negev.

Two ancient Nabatean towns, Avdat and Shivta, have been restored by the Israeli government. By excavating the ancient houses, farms, dams, wells, and other water-saving devices, modern experts have been learning how the Nabateans became such successful farmers.

The Nabatean civilization ended with the rise of Islam. From that time until the rise of the State of Israel many centuries later, the Negev was again left to the mercy of the desert.

LET PHARAOH FIND A WISE MAN

¹⁴Pharaoh sent for Yoseph, and they rushed him from the dungeon. He shaved, put on fresh clothes, and appeared before Pharaoh. ¹⁵"I have had a dream," Pharaoh said, "and no one can interpret it. But I have heard that you can interpret a dream the moment you hear it." ¹⁶"Not I," Yoseph replied to Pharaoh. "God will give Pharaoh an answer of peace."

²⁵Now Yoseph said to Pharaoh, "Pharaoh's dreams are really one. God has revealed to Pharaoh what He is about to do. ²⁶The seven healthy cows and the seven healthy ears are one dream, and its meaning: seven years of prosperity. ²⁷The seven skinny, ugly cows and the seven thin ears scorched by the east wind mean: seven years of famine. ²⁸It is just as I have told Pharaoh: God has revealed to Pharaoh what He is about to do.

---

15. BUT I HAVE HEARD THAT YOU CAN INTERPRET A DREAM THE MOMENT YOU HEAR IT.

וַאֲנִי שָׁמַעְתִּי עָלֶיךָ לֵאמֹר תִּשְׁמַע חֲלוֹם לִפְתֹּר אֹתוֹ

The word "hear" in "the moment you hear it" means both "to hear" and "to understand."

16. GOD WILL GIVE PHARAOH AN ANSWER OF PEACE.

אֱלֹהִים יַעֲנֶה אֶת־שְׁלוֹם פַּרְעֹה

Once again, Yoseph praises God as the source of all wisdom.

²⁹"The coming seven years will be ones of great prosperity in all the land of Egypt. ³⁰But these will be followed by seven years of famine, when all of the prosperity will be forgotten. Famine will devastate the land. ³³Therefore, let Pharaoh find a very wise man and put him in charge of all the land of Egypt. ³⁴Let Pharaoh take action, appoint officials throughout the country, and prepare Egypt by taking over one-fifth of all crops into storage during the seven prosperous years ahead. ³⁵Let them collect all the food of the good years ahead and store it away, under Pharaoh's authority, in the various towns. ³⁶The food shall be held in reserve for the country in preparation for the seven years of famine which shall come over the land of Egypt. In this way will the land survive the famine."

16. GOD WILL GIVE PHARAOH AN ANSWER OF PEACE.
אֱלֹהִים יַעֲנֶה אֶת־שְׁלוֹם פַּרְעֹה

Pharaoh had been upset ever since he had the dreams (verse 8). Now Yoseph assures him that the meaning will become clear and Pharaoh will again have peace of mind.

33. THEREFORE LET PHARAOH FIND A VERY WISE MAN.
וְעַתָּה יֵרֶא פַרְעֹה אִישׁ נָבוֹן וְחָכָם

The man chosen by Pharaoh must be able to rule the country fairly and peacefully during the difficult period ahead, and to know how to collect and store the grain so as to preserve it.

Joseph hoped Pharaoh would realize that he, Yoseph, was a man of understanding and wisdom, and would appoint him to this high position.

Answer the Questions

1. Who dreamed of seven fat and seven skinny cows?
2. How many dreams did Pharaoh have?
3. Who finally remembered Yoseph?
4. Who believed that Yoseph would give the Pharaoh the answer to his dream?
5. What was the meaning of the seven fat cows?
6. What was the meaning of the seven skinny cows?

What Do You Think?

1. What are the causes of famine?
2. Why was it necessary to find a wise man to take charge of the food?
3. Why did Yoseph suggest storing the food in many towns? Why not in one place?
4. Whom did Yoseph credit for his dream-solving skills?

Famines

It is hard for us to understand today how dreadful a famine can be, nor can we fully appreciate the constant concern of the ancients that they might soon have to face one. While there are several countries today in which people do not have enough food, they seem far away. And in our own country the poverty-stricken seem to find at least something.

We are fortunate to live in a country and climate where some things grow in every season, year-round, where refrigeration makes it possible to store food for long periods of time, and where rapid transportation makes it possible to ship large quantities of food from one place to another where it is needed. Modern science has made us much less dependent on the weather and the soil at any given time.

Ancient history records the effects on people who are dependent on nature for every drop of rain or an annual flooding of a river like the Nile to bring water for that year's crops. They, of course, had no way of knowing what the next year would bring, no less the next seven.

וַתִּכְלֶינָה שֶׁבַע שְׁנֵי הַשָּׂבָע אֲשֶׁר הָיָה בְּאֶרֶץ מִצְרָיִם

AND THE SEVEN YEARS OF FAMINE BEGIN

BERESHIT 41:39–53

³⁹Then Pharaoh said to Yoseph, "Since God has revealed all of this to you, there is no one as wise as you. ⁴⁰You shall therefore be in charge of my palace; and all my people shall obey your instructions. Only I, who am on the throne, shall be above you. ⁴¹I now put you in charge of the whole land of Egypt." ⁴²Taking the signet ring from his own hand, he put it on Yoseph's hand. ⁴⁵Then Pharaoh gave Yoseph the name "Zaphenath-paneah." And he gave him for a wife Asenath, the daughter of Poti-phera, priest of On.

---

40. ONLY I, WHO AM ON THE THRONE, SHALL BE ABOVE YOU. רַק הַכִּסֵּא אֶגְדַּל מִמֶּךָּ

"Only I, Pharaoh, will be mightier than you only by virtue of the fact that I am the crowned king of the land."

42. TAKING THE SIGNET RING FROM HIS HAND, HE PUT IT ON YOSEPH'S HAND. וַיָּסַר פַּרְעֹה אֶת־טַבַּעְתּוֹ מֵעַל יָדוֹ וַיִּתֵּן אֹתָהּ עַל־יַד־יוֹסֵף

He who received Pharaoh's ring was recognized as Pharaoh's chief minister.

⁴⁷During the next seven good years, the land produced rich crops. ⁴⁸So he collected food during the seven good years in the land of Egypt and stored in the cities what grew in the fields around each.

⁵⁰Before the years of famine came, Yoseph became the father of two sons, to whom Asenath, daughter of Poti-phera, the priest of On, gave birth. ⁵¹Yoseph named the first-born Manasseh, meaning, ''God has made me forget completely my hardships and my father's home.'' ⁵²He named the second one Ephraim, saying, ''God has made me fruitful in the land of my suffering.''

⁵³The seven years of plenty in the land of Egypt ended. ⁵⁴And the seven years of famine began, just as Yoseph had predicted. There was famine in all the countries. But in the land of Egypt, there was food.

---

45. THEN PHARAOH GAVE YOSEPH THE NAME ''ZAPHENATH-PANEAH.''

וַיִּקְרָא פַרְעֹה שֵׁם־יוֹסֵף צָפְנַת פַּעְנֵחַ

By giving Yoseph the signet ring, Pharaoh was giving him full authority to run the government. All royal documents were sealed with the signet ring.

Zaphenath-paneah may have these meanings: (1) food-man who brings life (2) revealer of secrets. Each meaning points to Yoseph's career, as the provider of food for people during the famine *and* the interpreter of dreams.

50. POTI-PHERA, THE PRIEST OF ON. פּוֹטִי פֶרַע כֹּהֵן אוֹן

Yoseph's father-in-law had the same name as his original Egyptian master, but the two were not the same man. On, which was later known as Heliopolis, was the center of worship of the sun-god, Ra.

53. THE SEVEN YEARS OF PLENTY IN THE LAND OF EGYPT.

שֶׁבַע שְׁנֵי הַשָּׂבָע אֲשֶׁר הָיָה בְּאֶרֶץ מִצְרָיִם

When the Nile River overflowed in the summer, the land was successfully farmed, and there were good crops.

Complete the Sentences

1. All my _____ shall obey your instructions.
2. Yoseph became the father of _____ sons.
3. Yoseph's first son was called _____.
4. Yoseph's second was called _____.
5. There was _____ in all the countries around Egypt.

t

two, people, Ephraim, Manasheh, famine

Answer the Questions

1. Who placed the signet ring on Yoseph's finger?
2. What was Yoseph's new name?
3. How many sons did Yoseph have?
4. What were the names of Yoseph's sons?

What Do You Think?

1. Why did Pharaoh choose Yoseph as the second-in-command?
2. What was the meaning of the signet ring?
3. How did Yoseph safeguard the land of Egypt?

LEADERS WORK HARD

1. Are you glad when you are picked to be a leader in your family, class, or other group?
2. Can you also be glad if someone else is picked to be a leader?
3. How can you help others be glad that you were picked to be a leader?

וְיוֹסֵף הוּא הַשַּׁלִיט עַל־הָאָרֶץ

YOSEPH WAS THE GOVERNOR OF THE LAND

BERESHIT
42:1–26

¹When Yaakov learned that there was grain available in Egypt, he said to his sons, "Why do you sit around staring at each other! ²I have heard that there is grain available in Egypt. Go down there and buy some for us, that we may live and not starve to death." ³So ten of Yoseph's brothers went down to Egypt to buy grain.

⁶Yoseph was the governor of the land. He was in charge of food-rationing for the whole population. It was to him that Yoseph's brothers also came, and they bowed low before him. ⁷When Yoseph saw his brothers, he recognized them immediately. But he acted like a stranger toward them and spoke harshly to them.

1. WHY DO YOU SIT AROUND STARING AT EACH OTHER! לָמָּה תִּתְרָאוּ

Yaakov saw grain being brought up from Egypt to Canaan by caravan. He was angry with his sons for not making the effort to go down to Egypt to buy food for their starving families.

2. GO DOWN THERE AND BUY SOME FOOD FOR US. רְדוּ־שָׁמָּה וְשִׁבְרוּ־לָנוּ מִשָּׁם

The Hebrew letters in the word רְדוּ ("go down") have a total numerical value of 210. This number corresponds to the number of years the children of Israel were to dwell in the land of Egypt. (See Gematria, page   .)

⁹And Yoseph remembered the dreams which he had once dreamed about them. So he said to them, "You are spies. You have come to search out the weakness of the land!" ¹⁰But they said to him, "No, my lord! Your servants have come only to buy food."

¹⁷And Yoseph had them arrested and put in jail for three days. ¹⁸On the third day, Yoseph said to them, "Do this and you shall live, for I am a God-fearing man. ¹⁹If you are really honest, then let one of you brothers remain here in jail, while the rest of you go and take home food for your starving families. ²⁰But you must bring back to me your youngest brother. In this way will the honesty of your words be proved, and you shall not die." They agreed. ²¹Then talking among themselves, they said, "Unfortunately, we are being punished because of what we did to our brother. We looked on as he suffered. When he pleaded with us, we would not listen."

²⁵Then Yoseph gave orders that their containers be filled with grain, that each one's money be returned to his sack, and that food be given to them for their return journey. All this was done for them. ²⁶They loaded their donkeys with the grain and they left for home.

---

9. AND YOSEPH REMEMBERED THE DREAMS THAT HE HAD ONCE DREAMED ABOUT THEM.

וַיִּזְכֹּר יוֹסֵף אֵת הַחֲלֹמוֹת אֲשֶׁר חָלַם לָהֶם

When Yoseph saw his brothers bow before him, he knew that the dream in which his brothers' sheaves had bowed to his sheaf was coming true.

Others say that Yoseph remembered that in the dream of the stars, the moon, and the sun, his father had bowed to him as well. Since this part of his dream still had not been fulfilled, Yoseph determined to bring his father down to Egypt.

21. UNFORTUNATELY, WE ARE BEING PUNISHED BECAUSE OF WHAT WE DID TO OUR BROTHER.

וְלֹא שָׁמַעְנוּ עַל־כֵּן בָּאָה אֵלֵינוּ הַצָּרָה הַזֹּאת

The brothers were recalling how cruelly they had treated young Yoseph. Now they were being repaid for that terrible wrong which they had done.

Complete the Sentences

1. I have heard that there is grain available in _____.
2. _____ of Yoseph's brothers went down to Egypt to buy grain.
3. Yoseph was the _____ of the land.
4. Yoseph remembered the _____ which he once dreamed.
5. We are being punished because of what we did to our _____.

dreams, ten, governor, Egypt, brother

Answer the Questions

1. Who urged the brothers to go to Egypt?
2. How many brothers went to Egypt?
3. Did Yoseph recognize his brothers?
4. Did Yoseph believe in God?
5. What was placed in the sacks of grain?

What Do You Think?

1. Why did Yaakov insist that his sons go down to Egypt to buy food?
2. Why did Yoseph make believe that he did not know his brothers?
3. Why did Yoseph give his brothers a taste of jail life?
4. Why did the brothers take double the money with them?
5. Did the brothers feel guilt for what they had done to Yoseph many years before?

Gematria גֵּמַטְרִיָּה

Gematria is a method for finding the hidden meaning of words and sentences in the Torah. It was developed by Jewish scholars in Talmudic times.

The word *Gematria* is of Greek origin. According to various theories, it is derived either from *geometria* (Greek for "geometry") or *grammateia* (Greek for "letter play"). The method is based upon the fact that each letter in the Hebrew alphabet is also a number. For example, א is 1, בּ is 2, ק is 100, תּ is 400, and so on. By adding up the numerical values of all the Hebrew letters in a word, phrase, or sentence, a hidden meaning is revealed.

For example, Yaakov dreamed about a stairway leading from earth to heaven. The letters in the word סֻלָּם, "stairway," add up to 130, the same total that we get if we add the values of the letters in סִינַי. This teaches us that the Torah, which was given on Mount Sinai, is the ladder between our earthly kingdom and God's kingdom in heaven.

The numerical value of the letters in אֶחָד ("one") is 13. By applying the technique of Gematria, we find that the letters in אַהֲבָה ("love") also add up to 13. This teaches us that the highest goal man can reach is love for God, who is One.

Here is the complete Hebrew alphabet and the numerical values for all the letters. Become a Gematria expert. What hidden meanings can you find in your name and the names of your relatives and friends? Use a Hebrew dictionary to find out the correct spellings of the names you are "analyzing."

ALEFBET NUMBER CHART

Alef	1	א	Het	8	ח	final Mem		ם	Tzadee	90	צ
Bet	2	בּ	Tet	9	ט	Nun	50	נ	final Tzadee		ץ
Vet		ב	Yod	10	י	final Nun		ן	Kof	100	ק
Gimel	3	ג	Kaf	20	כּ	Sameh	60	ס	Resh	200	ר
Dalet	4	ד	Haf		כ	Ayin	70	ע	Shin	300	שׁ
Hay	5	ה	final Haf		ך	Pay	80	פּ	Sin		שׂ
Vav	6	ו	Lamed	30	ל	Fay		פ	Tav	400	תּ
Zayin	7	ז	Mem	40	מ	final Fay		ף	Tav		ת

מַה־זֹּאת עָשָׂה אֱלֹהִים לָנוּ

WHAT HAS GOD DONE TO US?

27When they stopped to camp for the night, one of them opened his sack to feed his donkey. Suddenly, he saw his money in the sack. 28"Someone has returned my money!" he said to his brothers. "It is here in my sack!" Mystified, they turned to one another in fear and said, "What has God done to us?"

29When they came back to their father, Yaakov, in the land of Canaan, they told him all that had happened to them. 30"The man who is the head of the land," they said, "spoke harshly to us and charged us with spying on the country.

33"Then this man said to us, 'In this way will I know whether you are really honest men. Leave one of your brothers with me while the rest of you go home with food for your starving families. 34When you come back to me with your youngest brother, I will know that you are honest and that you are not spies. I will then restore your brother to you and you will be free to move about in the land.' "

---

28. SOMEONE HAS RETURNED MY MONEY! הוּשַׁב כַּסְפִּי

They did not know that Yoseph had ordered his servant to put the money they had paid for the grain back in their sacks. Now that they had discovered it, they were afraid that they would be accused of dishonesty.

28. WHAT HAS GOD DONE TO US?
מַה־זֹּאת עָשָׂה אֱלֹהִים לָנוּ

The brothers feared that the money had been placed in their sacks only to serve as a pretext for further accusations. Now they would be charged with being thieves as well as spies..

All About Dreams

Among the many interesting things which archaeologists discovered in Egypt was a "dream book" written in the 13th century B.C.E. Under the heading, "If a Man Sees Himself in a Dream," there are listed descriptions of all types of dreams, some good, some bad. According to this "dream book," wine usually has a good meaning. But birds are often a bad sign. The word for "bad" is written in this book in red, probably to suggest the color of blood.

Dreams, according to the Bible, were communications from God. This belief was carried forward into the later Talmudic period of Jewish history. Rabbi Chisda, one of the great teachers of the Talmud, said, "an uninterpreted dream is like an unread letter." In the Talmud tractate *Berachot*, considerable attention is given to the subject of dreams.

This is a prayer which is found in the traditional *Siddur*. It is part of the priestly blessing. The prayer reads,

"Lord of the Universe, I am Yours and my dreams are Yours. I have dreamed a dream and I do not know what it means. Whether I dream about myself, or I dream about others, if they be good dreams, strengthen them and fulfill them like the dreams of Yoseph. But if they need to be changed, heal them as the waters of Marah were healed by Moshe, our teacher, as Miryam was healed from her leprosy, as Hezekiah from his sickness, and as the waters of Yericho were sweetened by the hands Elisha. And as You turned the curse of the wicked Balaam into a blessing, so please turn all my dreams into good."

רִבּוֹנוֹ שֶׁל עוֹלָם, אֲנִי שֶׁלְּךָ וַחֲלוֹמוֹתַי שֶׁלָּךְ; חֲלוֹם חָלַמְתִּי וְאֵינִי יוֹדֵעַ מַה הוּא. יְהִי רָצוֹן מִלְּפָנֶיךָ, יְיָ אֱלֹהַי וֵאלֹהֵי אֲבוֹתַי, שֶׁיִּהְיוּ כָּל חֲלוֹמוֹתַי עָלַי וְעַל כָּל יִשְׂרָאֵל לְטוֹבָה, בֵּין שֶׁחָלַמְתִּי עַל עַצְמִי וּבֵין שֶׁחָלַמְתִּי עַל אֲחֵרִים וּבֵין שֶׁחָלְמוּ אֲחֵרִים עָלַי; אִם טוֹבִים הֵם, חַזְּקֵם וְאַמְּצֵם, וְיִתְקַיְּמוּ בִי וּבָהֶם כַּחֲלוֹמוֹת שֶׁל יוֹסֵף הַצַּדִּיק; וְאִם צְרִיכִים רְפוּאָה, רְפָאֵם כְּחִזְקִיָּהוּ מֶלֶךְ יְהוּדָה מֵחָלְיוֹ, וּכְמִרְיָם הַנְּבִיאָה מִצָּרַעְתָּהּ, וּכְנַעֲמָן מִצָּרַעְתּוֹ, וּכְמֵי מָרָה עַל יְדֵי מֹשֶׁה רַבֵּנוּ, וּכְמֵי יְרִיחוֹ עַל יְדֵי אֱלִישָׁע. וּכְשֵׁם שֶׁהָפַכְתָּ אֶת קִלְלַת בִּלְעָם הָרָשָׁע מִקְּלָלָה לִבְרָכָה, כֵּן תַּהֲפֹךְ כָּל חֲלוֹמוֹתַי עָלַי וְעַל כָּל יִשְׂרָאֵל לְטוֹבָה.

וְאֵל שַׁדַּי יִתֵּן לָכֶם רַחֲמִים

MAY ALMIGHTY GOD GIVE YOU FAVOR

BERESHIT 43:1–34

¹The famine in the land was more severe than ever. ²So when they had eaten up the grain which they had brought from Egypt, their father said to them, ''Go back again and get us some food.''

⁸Then Yehudah said to his father, Yisrael, ''Send the boy with me so that we may be on our way and save from death both you and ourselves, and our children.''

¹¹Now their father, Yisrael, finally said to them, ''If it must be so, then do this: Take some of the country's best products to that man as a gift. Take some balm, a supply of honey, spices, myrrh, pistachio nuts, and almonds. ¹²Also take double the money along, for you must return the money which was placed in your sacks by mistake. ¹³Take your brother, too, and go back to the man. ¹⁴May Almighty God give you favor with the man, that he may release your other brother and allow Binyamin's safe return.''

¹⁶When Yoseph saw Binyamin with them, he said to his chief servant, ''Take these men home. Have an animal slaughtered and prepared, for they will eat with me at noon.''

---

2. GO BACK AGAIN AND GET US SOME FOOD.
שֻׁבוּ שִׁבְרוּ־לָנוּ מְעַט־אֹכֶל

The Rabbis say that Yaakov was especially moved by the cries of his hungry little grandchildren.

26When Yoseph came home, they presented to him the gifts which they had, and they bowed low before him. 27After he greeted them, he asked, "And how is your father, the old man about whom you spoke last time. Is he well?" 28"Your servant, our father, is alive and well," they answered. And they bowed low before him. 29As Yoseph looked around, he saw his brother Binyamin, his own mother's son. He asked, "Is this your youngest brother, of whom you spoke to me?" He kept himself under control and gave the order, "Serve the meal!"

34Yoseph had portions served to them from his own table. But Binyamin's servings were five times as large as any of the others. They drank and had a wonderful time with Yoseph.

---

11. SOME BALM. מְעַט צֳרִי

Balm was a pleasant-smelling resin obtained from certain trees and used in perfumes. Honey was made from dates. Myrrh was also a resin from trees that was used in making incense.

12. AND TAKE DOUBLE THE MONEY.
וְכֶסֶף מִשְׁנֶה קְחוּ בְיֶדְכֶם

Thinking that prices might have risen in the meantime, the brothers took twice as much money as on their first journey to Egypt.

34. BINYAMIN'S SERVINGS WERE FIVE TIMES AS LARGE.
וַתֵּרֶב מַשְׂאַת בִּנְיָמִין מִמַּשְׂאֹת כֻּלָּם חָמֵשׁ יָדוֹת

Yoseph would use this meal as a way of testing his brothers. He would give Binyamin much larger portions than the others, to see whether his brothers would become jealous of him.

Complete the Sentence

1. He saw his brother _____, his own mother's son.
2. Binyamin's portions were _____ times as large as any of the others.
3. You must return the _____ which was placed in your sacks.
4. The _____ in the land was more severe than ever.
5. Their father said, "Go back and get us some_____."

money, Binyamin, food, famine, five

Who Said It?

1. Go back and get us some food _____.
2. Send the boy with me _____.
3. Take these men home _____
4. How is your father? _____.

What Do You Think?

1. Why did Yaakov insist that the brothers return to Egypt?
2. Did Yaakov want to send Binyamin to Egypt? Why not?
3. Why did the brothers take twice as much money as they needed?
4. Why was Binyamin given more food than any of the others?

Choosing Between Good and Evil

There was a great battle being fought inside Yoseph's mind and heart. The army of good was defending itself against the soldiers of evil. The army of evil pressured Yoseph, "These are the no-goodniks who sold you as a slave. Give them a dose of their own medicine. Get even! Lower the boom on them!"

The army of good argued, "Let by-gones be by-gones. Forgive and forget. It's time for a new beginning."

In Yoseph's case the army of good creamed the evil ones.

The good side is called יֵצֶר הַטּוֹב (*yetzer hatov*), and the bad side, יֵצֶר הָרַע (*yetzer hara*). The *tov* side says, "Be good, be kind," but the *ra* says, "Be selfish, be mean!" And so the *tov* and *ra* are always fighting, each one trying to have its own way.

But it's up to *you* to choose. Many times you have to choose between something wrong that seems like fun and something right that seems like a real drag. And the people who are close to you—your family, your friends—will have an important influence on your choice. "Everybody's doing it, and "You're not chicken, are you?" are phrases that should warn you that your friend is trying to convince you to do wrong. That's why it's so important to choose your friends carefully. A good friend will help you to choose right, and a bad friend will lead you to do wrong.

Sometimes the choice between good and evil may not really be clear to you. Suppose your best friend told you he had to pass an important test or he would fail the course and have to go to summer school. He wouldn't be able to go to summer camp, and his family would be awfully mad! If he wanted you to give him the test answers, what would you do? That would be a good problem to discuss with someone whose opinion you can trust—maybe your mother or father. They might suggest that you help your friend by tutoring him *before* the exam so that he would be able to pass by himself. He would feel better if he passed honestly, too.

That's the big difference between *tov* and *ra*. When you listen to the *tov* and do the right thing, you feel great! But if you do what the *ra* says, you feel guilty and find that you don't like yourself. The choice is up to you!

לָמָה שִׁלַּמְתֶּם רָעָה תַּחַת טוֹבָה

WHY DID YOU DO WRONG IN RETURN FOR GOOD?

**BERESHIT
44:1–20**

¹Yoseph now gave orders to the manager of his palace, saying, ''Fill the men's sacks with as much food as they can hold, and put in each man's sack the money he has paid. ²But in the bag of the youngest son, put my silver goblet, along with the money which he paid for his grain.'' So the manager did as Yoseph had instructed him.

³Then, in the very early morning, at dawn, the men were sent off with their donkeys. ⁴They had not gone very far out of the city when Yoseph said to his manager, ''Get up and follow those men! When you reach them, ask them, 'Why did you do wrong in return for good? ⁵Why did you take the silver goblet from which my master drinks and which he uses for divination? It was a terrible wrong that you did!' ''

¹¹Each of them quickly lowered his bag to the ground and opened it. ¹²A search was made, beginning with the oldest and ending with the youngest. The cup was found in Binyamin's sack. ¹³They ripped their clothes in despair. Then each of them reloaded his donkey and they returned to the city.

¹⁴Yoseph was still at home when Yehudah and his brothers reentered his house. ¹⁵Then Yoseph said to them, ''What kind of business is this! Certainly you should have known that I have my special way of discovering things.'' ¹⁷But Yoseph said, ''That is not my way of doing things. Only the man with whom the goblet was found shall become my slave.''

¹⁸Now Yehudah approached him and said, ²⁰My lord, ''We have an old father and a young brother, the child of his old age. His own brother is dead, and he alone is left of his mother's children. He is our father's favorite.''

---

14. YOSEPH WAS STILL AT HOME.
יוֹסֵף וְהוּא עוֹדֶנּוּ שָׁם

Yoseph had no mind for anything else that day except this carefully planned drama with his brothers. He stayed home and waited for their return.

17. ONLY THE MAN WITH WHOM THE GOBLET IS FOUND SHALL BECOME MY SLAVE.
הוּא אֲשֶׁר יִמָּצֵא אִתּוֹ יִהְיֶה־לִּי עָבֶד

Yoseph did all this to test his brothers, to learn whether they would be willing to risk danger in order to save their brother Binyamin, Yoseph remembered how eagerly his brothers had betrayed him, and wanted to see whether they would do the same to Binyamin.

20. HIS OWN BROTHER IS DEAD. וְאָחִיו מֵת
Yehudah spoke of Joseph as being dead.

Complete the Sentences

1. In the bag of the _____ son put my silver goblet.
2. The cup was found in Benjamin's _____.
3. Fill the men's sacks with as much _____ as they can hold.
4. Only the man with whom the goblet was found shall be my _____.

slave, youngest, sack, food

Answer the Questions

1. In whose bag did they find the silver goblet?
2. What two things were placed in the sacks?
3. What was the silver goblet used for?
4. Whom did Yoseph wish to keep as a slave?
5. Who was Yaakov's favorite son?

What Do You Think?

1. Why did Yoseph place the goblet in Binyamin's sack?
2. Why was Yoseph playing games with his brothers?
3. Why did Yehudah mention his dead brother?
4. How do you think Yoseph reacted when Yehudah sorrowfully said "his dead brother"?

Communication

There is a word which we should all remember, for it is a powerful word. That word is *communicate*. To communicate means to give or send some kind of message. When we talk with people, we communicate with them. When they talk with us, they communicate with us.

But real communication is a two-sided coin. It takes not only talking, but listening too. We should all try to be good listeners and to communicate in a way that invites others to listen to us.

Yoseph could not decide whether to communicate directly with the brothers and tell them that he was their long-lost brother. He kept testing to find out whether they were really sorry for the crime they had committed. From their conversation Yoseph learned that they were truly sorry and that they felt they were now being repaid for the crime they had committed.

If only they had taken the time years before to talk, to communicate with their brother Yoseph, then perhaps things could have been different.

Communication among family members is especially important. If the brothers had discussed their problem with Yoseph, perhaps he would have changed and the problem could have been avoided. When you communicate you can avoid lots of misunderstandings.

Perhaps if Yaakov had talked to Yoseph about his bragging, the brothers would have been friendlier with each other.

Describe how you would tell your family about the following:

1. How would you tell your family that you broke something special?

2. How would you tell your family that you love them?

3. How would you tell your family that you aren't feeling well?

4. How would you tell your family that you need their help?

5. How would you tell your family that your Hebrew teacher wants them to come to school?

6. How would you tell your family that you need more time alone?

אֲנִי יוֹסֵף
I AM YOSEPH

BERESHIT 45:1–28 ¹Yoseph could no longer control himself, so he cried out to his attendants, "Get out, all of you, from before me!" ³"I am Yoseph!" he said to his brothers. "And my father is still alive!" But his brothers said nothing to him; they were so stunned by this. ⁴"Come closer to me," Yoseph told them. So they came closer to him. He spoke again, "I am Yoseph, your brother whom you sold into Egypt.

1. YOSEPH COULD NO LONGER CONTROL HIMSELF.
וְלֹא־יָכֹל יוֹסֵף לְהִתְאַפֵּק

Hearing the brothers mention the sadness and tragedy of his father, Yaakov, Yoseph could no longer hold on to his emotion. The moment had come when he must reveal himself to his brothers. It was to be between him and them, a family matter, and Yoseph wanted privacy.

1. GET OUT, ALL OF YOU. הוֹצִיאוּ כָל־אִישׁ מֵעָלָי

Yoseph ordered all his servants to leave the room so that his brothers would not be put to shame before them when the truth was revealed; namely, that they had sold Yoseph into slavery.

4. I AM YOSEPH, YOUR BROTHER, WHOM YOU SOLD INTO EGYPT.
אֲנִי יוֹסֵף אֲחִיכֶם אֲשֶׁר־מְכַרְתֶּם אֹתִי מִצְרָיְמָה

This should prove to you that I am really Yoseph, for beside yourselves no one else but Yoseph would know that Yoseph had been sold into slavery.

⁵But don't be angry with yourselves that you sold me here. It was really God who sent me ahead of you to help save life."

¹⁶When the news reached Pharaoh's palace, "Yoseph's brothers have come," Pharaoh and his court were pleased. ¹⁷And Pharaoh said to Yoseph, "Tell your brothers, 'This is what you are to do: Load up your animals and go back immediately to the land of Canaan. ¹⁸Take your father and all of your families and come to me. I will give to you some of the best territory of Egypt, where you shall live off the fat of the land."

²¹The sons of Yisrael did as they were told.

²⁵They left Egypt and went back to their father, Yaakov, in the land of Canaan. ²⁶And they told him, "Yoseph is still alive, and he is ruler over the whole land of Egypt!" Yaakov's heart stood still, for he did not believe them. ²⁷But when they had given him all of Yoseph's messages, and when he saw the wagons that Yoseph had sent for his journey, their father, Yaakov, came alive. ²⁸"Enough," said Yisrael. "My son Yoseph is still alive! I will go and see him before I die."

---

5. IT WAS REALLY GOD WHO SENT ME AHEAD OF YOU TO HELP SAVE LIFE.

לְמִחְיָה שְׁלָחַנִי אֱלֹהִים לִפְנֵיכֶם

Yoseph was being superbly generous, urging his brothers to drop the blame from themselves and accept all that had happened as God's doing for the good of all.

28. I WILL GO AND SEE HIM BEFORE I DIE.

אֵלְכָה וְאֶרְאֶנּוּ בְּטֶרֶם אָמוּת

Yaakov's original intention was to visit Yoseph for a while, but not to settle in the land of Egypt, for he loved the land of Canaan too much to want to leave it for good.

Complete the Sentences

1. I am _____ your brother.
2. It was really _____ who sent me ahead of you.
3. Take your _____ and all your families and come to me.
4. I will give you some of the best territories in _____.
5. My _____ Yoseph is alive.

father, God, Yoseph, Egypt, son

Answer the Questions

1. Why did Yoseph command his servants to leave him?
2. Why was the Pharaoh so good to Yoseph's family?

What Do You Think?

1. Should Yoseph have taken revenge on his brothers?
2. What makes you think that Yaakov did not trust his own sons?
3. What convinced Yaakov that the sons were telling him the truth?

Yoseph Reveals His Identity

Yehudah offered a moving plea to this mysterious man who held their lives in his power. He begged him to have mercy on their old father, for Binyamin had been his particularly beloved son ever since the death of another brother. Yehudah pleaded that he be made a slave but that Binyamin be allowed his freedom to return home. Finally, Yoseph was convinced that brotherly love now existed among them. There was no need for further challenges to his brothers.

Yoseph ordered all of his staff to leave at once, and he remained alone with his unhappy brothers. He then revealed to them his true identity. He was none other than Yoseph, their brother!

In the early Biblical story of humankind, one brother killed the other. When his crime was about to be discovered he cried out: "Am I my brother's keeper?" The Bible leaves the answer to be filled in by each and every one of us. God wants people to answer, "Yes indeed, I am my brother's keeper."

1. Do all sisters and brothers run into difficulties with one another?
2. What happens when differences arise between sisters and brothers?
3. How do we resolve such differences?

וְאָנֹכִי אַעַלְךָ גַם עָלֹה

I WILL BRING YOU UP AGAIN

BERESHIT
46:1–30

¹So Yisrael set out on his journey with everything that he had; and he came to Beer-sheva, where he offered sacrifices to the God of his father, Yitzchak. ²During the night, God spoke to Yisrael in a vision. "Yaakov! Yaakov!" He called. And Yaakov answered, "Here I am."
⁴"I will go down with you to Egypt, and I will also bring you up again. And Yoseph will be close to you when you die." ⁵So Yaakov left Beer-sheva, and the sons of Yisrael brought their father Yaakov, their children, and their wives in the wagons Pharaoh had sent to carry them.

---

1. SO YISRAEL SET OUT ON HIS JOURNEY WITH EVERYTHING THAT HE HAD AND HE CAME TO BEER-SHEBA.

וַיִּסַּע יִשְׂרָאֵל וְכָל־אֲשֶׁר־לוֹ וַיָּבֹא בְּאֵרָה שָּׁבַע

Yaakov (Yisrael) had been living in Hevron. He now began the journey southward to Egypt, stopping off at Beer-sheva.

2. DURING THE NIGHT, GOD SPOKE TO YISRAEL IN A VISION.

וַיֹּאמֶר אֱלֹהִים לְיִשְׂרָאֵל בְּמַרְאֹת הַלַּיְלָה

"In a night-time vision" would mean in a dream.

4. I WILL GO DOWN WITH YOU TO EGYPT, AND I WILL ALSO BRING YOU UP AGAIN.

אָנֹכִי אֵרֵד עִמְּךָ מִצְרַיְמָה וְאָנֹכִי אַעַלְךָ גַם עָלֹה

God made two promises here: (1) Yaakov would be buried in Canaan when he died, and (2) God would someday bring back Yaakov's descendants from Egypt to Canaan.

Yaakov could die in peace in Egypt because his beloved son Yoseph would be right by him for the rest of Yaakov's life.

[7]He brought with him to Egypt his sons and grandsons, his daughters and granddaughters—all of his descendants. [26]All the people who came with Yaakov to Egypt, not counting the wives of Yaakov's sons, numbered sixty-six descendants. [27]With Yoseph's two sons who were born in Egypt, the complete family of Yaakov in Egypt was seventy people. [29]Yoseph ordered his chariot, and went up to Goshen to meet his father. When he met him, they embraced each other and wept a long time. [30]And Yisrael said to Yoseph, "Now I can die, for I have seen you in person and know that you are indeed alive!"

[23]Then Yoseph said to the people, "I have now gotten your land for Pharaoh. Here is your seed. Go and sow the land."

BERESHIT
47:23

---

26. ALL THE PEOPLE WHO CAME WITH YAAKOV TO EGYPT, NOT COUNTING THE WIVES OF YAAKOV'S SONS, NUMBERED SIXTY-SIX DESCENDANTS.

כָּל הַנֶּפֶשׁ הַבָּאָה לְיַעֲקֹב מִצְרַיְמָה יֹצְאֵי יְרֵכוֹ מִלְּבַד נְשֵׁי בְנֵי־יַעֲקֹב כָּל

נֶפֶשׁ שִׁשִּׁים וָשֵׁשׁ

Leah's descendants were thirty-three, Zilpah's sixteen, Rachel's fourteen, and Bilhah's seven. These together add up to a total of seventy. If Erd and Onan, who died in Canaan, and Manasseh and Ephraim, who were born in Egypt, are excluded, then the total adds up to sixty-six who made the journey from Canaan to Egypt.

27. THE COMPLETE FAMILY OF YAAKOV WAS SEVENTY PEOPLE.

כָּל־הַנֶּפֶשׁ לְבֵית־יַעֲקֹב הַבָּאָה מִצְרַיְמָה שִׁבְעִים

Sixty-six people left Canaan. By the time they reached Egypt, their number had grown to seventy, since Yoseph and his two sons, and Yocheved, who was born just as the clan entered Egypt, were added to the original sixty-six.

Others explain that Yaakov himself was counted as the seventieth person.

Complete the Sentences

1. I will go down to _____ with you.
2. And _____ will be close to you when you die.
3. The complete family of Yaakov, in Egypt, was _____ people.
4. Here is your _____ . Go and sow the land.

Answer the Questions

1. Where did Yisrael offer sacrifices to God?
2. What did God promise Yisrael?
3. How many people were in Yaakov's complete family?
4. Where did Yoseph meet his father Yaakov?

What Do You Think

1. What is meant by the phrase "I will bring you up again"?
2. How did Pharaoh show his respect for Yaakov?

Yaakov's Family Tree

According to the Midrash, Yoseph's sons, who had grown up in Egypt, could easily have chosen to remain Egyptians. Nevertheless, Ephraim and Manasheh chose to be Hebrews and became part of Yaakov's family.

Yaakov saw the Hebrew loyalty and adopted them as his very own children.

Your Family Tree

The Bible tells us about the human family. It recorded the family tree of humankind by tracing it to Noah and his three sons. According to the Torah, the descendants of Shem populated the Fertile Crescent of Asia. Those of Ham became the peoples of Egypt and other nearby African lands. The descendants of Japhet made up all the nations of Asia Minor and the inland peoples of the Mediterranean.

In Jewish tradition families are very important. The celebration of Shabbat and the holidays revolve around family observances. We stay home, enjoying the company of our families. We visit, and are visited by, uncles, cousins, and aunts, and other relatives.

Family members are important to us. In times of joy they celebrate with us and share our happiness. In times of trouble we turn to them for help and advice. In times of sorrow they share our sadness.

Happy, sharing families are a treasure beyond compare.

The study of family ancestry and history is called genealogy. A genealogist who is tracing a family makes a drawing that looks like a tree. This family tree has a thick trunk, strong limbs, small branches, and tiny leaves.

Become your family's genealogist. Record the names of your family and the relatives on your father's and mother's sides of the family. If you can, do not forget to record their Hebrew names.

Call on your parents to help you.

קִבְרוּ אֹתִי אֶל־אֲבֹתָי

LET ME SLEEP WITH MY ANCESTOR

²⁷Now Yisrael lived in the land of Goshen in Egypt. They became prosperous and their numbers grew quickly. ²⁸Yaakov lived seventeen years in the land of Egypt, and the length of his life was 147 years. ²⁹When the time came close for Yisrael to die, he called for his son Yoseph and said to him, "If you truly love me, make me a solemn promise, a pledge of your loyalty, that you will not bury me in Egypt. ³⁰But let me sleep with my ancestors. Carry me up from Egypt and bury me in their burial-place."

30. BUT LET ME SLEEP WITH MY ANCESTORS.
וְשָׁכַבְתִּי עִם־אֲבֹתַי
Yaakov wanted to be buried in Canaan, in the Cave of Machpelah, where Avraham and Yitzchak were buried.

²⁹Then he instructed them, saying, "I am about to die. Bury me with my fathers in the cave which is in the field of Ephron the Hittite, ³⁰the cave in the field of Machpelah, facing Mamre in the land of Canaan, which Avraham bought from Ephron the Hittite for a burial place."

³³When Yaakov had finished his instructions to his sons, he drew his feet into bed, breathed his last, and died.

¹⁴After burying his father, Yoseph returned to Egypt, together with his brothers and all who had gone up with him to bury his father.

²⁵Then Yoseph made the sons of —Yisrael swear, saying, "When God remembers you, be sure to carry up my body from here."

²⁶Yoseph died at the age of 110 years. He was embalmed and placed in a coffin in Egypt.

14. YOSEPH RETURNED TO EGYPT TOGETHER WITH HIS BROTHERS AND ALL WHO HAD GONE UP WITH HIM.

וַיָּשָׁב יוֹסֵף מִצְרַיְמָה הוּא וְאֶחָיו וְכָל־הָעֹלִים אִתּוֹ

The Egyptians, who saw the great respect paid by the kings of Canaan to Yaakov, now honored Yoseph and his family even more.

25. BE SURE TO CARRY UP MY BODY FROM HERE.

וְהַעֲלִתֶם אֶת־עַצְמֹתַי מִזֶּה

When the Jews finally left Egypt, Moshe himself took Yoseph's coffin from the land, fulfilling his last wish.

26. YOSEPH DIED AT THE AGE OF 110 YEARS. HE WAS EMBALMED AND PLACED IN A COFFIN IN EGYPT.

וַיָּמָת יוֹסֵף בֶּן־מֵאָה וָעֶשֶׂר שָׁנִים וַיַּחַנְטוּ אֹתוֹ וַיִּישֶׂם בָּאָרוֹן בְּמִצְרָיִם

With Yoseph's death, the period of the Patriarchs was ended.

Complete the Sentences

1. Bury me in the cave which is in the field of _____.
2. After burying his father, _____ returned to Egypt.
3. Be sure to carry up my _____ from here.
4. Yoseph died at the age of _____ years.

Yoseph, 110, Ephron the Hittite, body

Answer the Questions

1. Where was the cave of Machpelah?
2. Who bought the field of Machpelah from Ephron the Hittite?
3. Where did the brothers go after they buried Yaakov?

What Do You Think?

1. Was it necessary for Yaakov to emphasize that the field had been purchased?
2. What did Yaakov mean by the phrase "When God remembers you"?
3. How did God remember the Jewish people in 1948?
4. What is meant by the phrase "he drew his feet into bed"?

The Death of Yoseph

When Yaakov died, the brothers were worried that Yoseph might again recall the wrong which they had done to him long ago. But Yoseph assured them that everything that had happened had turned out for the best. It had been God's will and they ought not to blame themselves. He had surely forgiven them for their wrongdoing.

The years passed by and Yoseph together with his brothers grew old. When Yoseph's time for dying came close, he asked of his brothers that when they or their descendants someday in the future return to the land of their fathers in Canaan, they would take along his remains for burial in the country of their birth.

Death marks the end of the journey called life. It comes to everything in nature: plant life, animal life, human life, to all alike. The Psalmist of the Bible summarized it well when he wrote that man is "like grass which grows up in the morning but with the coming of evening it fades and withers away" (Psalms 90:5–6). Another Biblical writer put it this way: "One generation goes and another generation comes but the world continues on" (Ecclesiastes 1:4). Life is a treasure which is passed on to those who follow us.

1. Why was Yoseph eager to be buried in Canaan?
2. Have you ever visited a cemetery? What was your reaction?
3. Why did Yoseph want his body taken from Egypt?